SUPPORTING TEACHER \

All teachers are in the unique position of influencing the future happiness and success of the next generation; therefore it is crucial that the wellbeing of teachers is not overlooked. This proactive guide will empower school staff; it will enlighten and equip them with essential knowledge about wellbeing and remind them to never neglect their own health. It encourages a proactive approach to holistic wellbeing and deals with a serious topic in a humorous and lighthearted way.

Structured as an easy-to-read guide, the chapters offer hands-on tips on how and why to support teacher wellbeing and advice on how to manage the increasing demands of planning, assessment and marking. What's more, it emphasises the importance of sustaining a work-life balance, using mindfulness to relax and gain perspective, healthy eating, incorporating exercise into your schedule and maintaining a sense of calm in the classroom. This book:

- Includes personal stories that encompass the real experiences of early-career teachers, experienced teachers, senior leaders and trainee teachers.
- Delves into important topics such as stress, burnout, work-life balance, anxiety and controlling the mind.
- Highlights how to increase self-esteem, confidence and eradicate perfectionism at work.
- Suggests practical strategies related to workload reduction, peer support and a variety of self-care techniques.

Written by a Primary Education lecturer with over 20 years of experience teaching in primary schools, this book is an essential resource for trainee teachers, early-career teachers, experienced teachers and school leaders alike.

Suzanne Allies is a Senior Lecturer at the University of Worcester. She has taught in Higher Education for eight years and as a primary teacher for 20 years. Her main passion is to encourage and support the mental health and wellbeing of teachers, trainee teachers, children and adolescents.

'This book provides a practical and reflective tool to support teachers and childcare professionals in evaluating and developing their physical, emotional and mental wellbeing. Its warm and readable style makes it accessible to those in whatever stage of wellbeing they find themselves. Peppered with examples from personal experience and professional practice, it offers a range of structures and resources to promote wellbeing within the children's workforce. Most helpfully, it gives us permission to engage with these issues, whatever our role in the education system.'

—Professor Richard Woolley, Deputy Head of the School of Education, University of Worcester

'As teachers, we rightly put the needs of each child first, but often neglect our own wellbeing. This book is a fantastic resource for school leaders to use personally, as well as for staff, written by someone who has been there herself. The case study examples resound, and the takeaway messages of each chapter help you reflect on your own practice.'

—Spencer Morris, Headteacher of Red Hill C of E Primary School

SUPPORTING TEACHER WELLBEING

A Practical Guide for Primary Teachers and School Leaders

Suzanne Allies

Routledge
Taylor & Francis Group
LONDON AND NEW YORK

First published 2021
by Routledge
2 Park Square, Milton Park, Abingdon, Oxon OX14 4RN

and by Routledge
52 Vanderbilt Avenue, New York, NY 10017

Routledge is an imprint of the Taylor & Francis Group, an informa business

© 2021 Suzanne Allies

The right of Suzanne Allies to be identified as author of this work has been asserted by her in accordance with sections 77 and 78 of the Copyright, Designs and Patents Act 1988.

All rights reserved. No part of this book may be reprinted or reproduced or utilised in any form or by any electronic, mechanical, or other means, now known or hereafter invented, including photocopying and recording, or in any information storage or retrieval system, without permission in writing from the publishers.

Trademark notice: Product or corporate names may be trademarks or registered trademarks, and are used only for identification and explanation without intent to infringe.

British Library Cataloguing-in-Publication Data
A catalogue record for this book is available from the British Library

Library of Congress Cataloging-in-Publication Data

Names: Allies, Suzanne, author.
Title: Supporting teacher wellbeing : a practical guide for primary teachers and school leaders / Suzanne Allies.
Identifiers: LCCN 2020020255 | ISBN 9780367353247 (hardback) | ISBN 9780367353254 (paperback) | ISBN 9780429330698 (ebook)
Subjects: LCSH: Teachers--Mental health. | Teachers--Job stress. | Burn out (Psychology)--Prevention. | Teaching--Psychological aspects.
Classification: LCC LB2840 .A45 2021 | DDC 371.102--dc23
LC record available at https://lccn.loc.gov/2020020255

ISBN: 978-0-367-35324-7 (hbk)
ISBN: 978-0-367-35325-4 (pbk)
ISBN: 978-0-429-33069-8 (ebk)

Typeset in Joanna
by SPi Global, India

CONTENTS

Acknowledgements vi
About the author vii

Introduction 1

PART 1: UNDERSTANDING WELLBEING 9

1 Why should teachers support their mental
   health and wellbeing? 11
2 What do you need to know about wellbeing? 32

PART 2: STRATEGIES FOR WELLBEING 59

3 Which work-life balance strategies best support wellbeing? 61
4 What other strategies support teacher wellbeing? 84

PART 3: A PERSONAL PLAN FOR WELLBEING 123

5 How can you plan for sustained teacher wellbeing? 125
6 What is my personal plan for wellbeing? 157

References 177
Index 186

ACKNOWLEDGEMENTS

I'd like to dedicate this book to my Poppy (31st Dec 2002–21st May 2014)

I want to mention thanks to my husband, Neil, for proofreading my chapters so diligently and honestly. Thanks always to my daughters, Charlie and Georgia, who constantly inspire me. Thanks to my editor, Bruce Roberts, for granting me the opportunity to write a book about a subject that means so much to me.

I would like to thank the following people who inspired the personal reflections I make throughout:

Bryony Baynes, Megan Crosby, Amandine Stone, Karen Bubb, Rachael Paige, Greg Clarke, Ali Elwell, Derval Carey-Jenkins, Andy Hale, Sharon Lannie, Kerry Richards, Fiona Davies, Kelsang Khechog, Louisa Gwillym, Petr Horacek, Holly Guest, Tina Salisbury, Jane Ellis-Tate and Andrew Morley.

'When it rains, look for rainbows, when it's dark, look for stars' (Oscar Wilde).

ABOUT THE AUTHOR

Suzanne Allies is a Senior Lecturer at the University of Worcester and has taught in Higher Education for eight years. She has 20 years of teaching experience in primary schools and was PSHE coordinator for over 10 years in a three-form entry primary school. Suzanne is wellbeing coordinator at her university and has led on many initiatives, such as securing the funding to provide students with art therapy sessions that they can use in school to support mental health in the classroom. Currently, she is Module Leader for an innovative undergraduate module, Developing Self, which encourages students to reflect on their personal, academic and professional selves. This module supports the students' social and emotional student wellbeing as a priority, covering topics such as work-life balance and resilience. Suzanne's true passion is for supporting the mental health and wellbeing of university students, teachers and children. She has delivered many Staff Wellbeing workshops in a range of primary schools. She has presented on 'Wellbeing' at the 2018 NaPTEC conference where she spoke about mindfulness in schools (having been a Buddhist practitioner for 10 years). She is a Youth Mental Health First Aid (MHFA England) Instructor, and has trained in both a Level 2 in counselling skills and a Level 3 in counselling studies. She is a

Crisis Volunteer for the crisis text-line Shout, a Champion for Time to Change and an Advisor for Mind's Mentally Healthy Universities. Suzanne's master's dissertation focused on the perceptions and attitudes that personal tutors have towards supporting the mental health of students. She has formed a Staff Mental Health Network at the University of Worcester which is expanding rapidly and ensuring that staff mental health is prioritized and brought to the forefront of discussions. Suzanne is also a qualified beauty therapist and masseur.

INTRODUCTION

Why I'm writing this book

To fulfil your potential as a teacher, it is crucial to maintain a focus on yourself and your wellbeing. This may seem an impossible task on busy teaching days, but this book will show you that good wellbeing is always within your reach and can be accomplished in a few easy steps. The content has been designed to guide and inform teachers and school leaders to prioritise wellbeing in an inclusive, caring and non-stigmatising way. My passionate hope is for you to learn from my mistakes and to benefit from my knowledge about how best to support teacher wellbeing. Personal recounts throughout this book are differentiated using italic font and text boxes. These recounts are stories and reflections that detail both personal struggles and positive experiences; they are often mine, but there are also stories from teachers and leaders in school. It is hoped that these stories might resonate with you in some way. However, I am conscious of not making this book 'all about me'. Therefore, feel free to skip over the sections in italics and text boxes if you wish, and focus only on the science of wellbeing!

I neglected my own wellbeing for over 15 years as a teacher as I attempted, and failed, to juggle work and family life. After a brief absence from work due to stress, I returned to teach with a renewed sense of purpose. Fortunately, I had identified a range of wellbeing strategies to have at my disposal that allowed me to function more productively and with my wellbeing placed center-stage. My new motto became: My health comes first.

The structure of this book

This book is comprised of three parts:

Part 1: Understanding wellbeing:

- definitions and the meaning of wellbeing,
- supporting your own wellbeing,
- supporting the wellbeing of colleagues,
- education and wellbeing,
- the theoretical underpinning and science behind wellbeing.

Part 2: Strategies for wellbeing:

- practical ideas about how to support wellbeing,
- how to achieve more work-life balance,
- two stories of early-career teachers related to work-life balance,
- issues related to workload, particularly around planning, preparation and marking,
- the part that self-esteem, resilience and perfectionism can play in wellbeing,
- wellbeing strategies related to sleep, mindfulness, healthy eating and exercise.

Part 3: A personal plan for wellbeing:

- guidance for school leaders in promoting whole-school staff wellbeing,
- wellbeing initiatives linked to a school's ethos and values,
- a personal plan (called 'Steps to Success'),
- A staff wellbeing action plan for school leaders,
- effectively communicating with staff about wellbeing,
- formulating a staff wellbeing policy.

How to use this book

This book will guide you towards building the reserves and strategies you need to teach and stay happy and committed to your rewarding, yet challenging, job. When I talk about staying happy, I don't mean that you will be skipping through fields of daisies and permanently feeling content and relaxed (although you might!). I am referring to a basic feeling of 'everything being okay' in your daily job. This realistic idea of happiness also means you will experience a sense of purpose and many moments of pleasure and satisfaction in your life.

I don't want you to approach this book as a 'quick fix' to happiness and wellbeing because such a thing does not exist. When you fixate on striving for happiness, you soon find out that happiness is elusive and ever-changing (often for no reason). In fact, the word 'happiness' comes from the Middle English word 'hap', meaning chance or good luck. Whippman (2016) states that the more relentlessly we value and pursue happiness, the more likely we are to be depressed, anxious and lonely.

Unfortunately, we never know what is around the corner and having a preventative and proactive approach to our wellbeing makes more sense than a reactive approach for those trickier times. 'Wellbeing' is a more realistic and representative way to describe being happy. All of us can achieve wellbeing by getting to know ourselves better and working out how small changes, such as a deep breath occasionally when we feel tense, can make a big difference. A variety of practices and mindsets will be suggested within this book so you can find a wellbeing path that suits you perfectly. The secret is to find things that support your personal wellbeing needs that are sustainable in the long-term.

I have tried to provide a holistic approach to wellbeing. I use the terms 'staff', 'teachers' and 'colleagues' interchangeably throughout, but the guidance I offer is suited to all employees working in a school. Please forgive me for any omissions, as I cannot claim to know everything there is to know about supporting wellbeing! You may like to arm yourself with a highlighter pen so that you can mark the strategies that could work for you. You will instinctively begin to know how to achieve wellbeing for yourself, and which strategies are worth trying and which you can ignore. Teamwork is paramount for the wellbeing of the whole school, so, if you do find any strategies in this book that work well for you, it may be worth sharing these at work. **All the figures featured in this book can be downloaded from my website: www.supportingteacherwellbeing.wordpress.com**

Steps to success

There is a template in Chapter 6 (Figure 6.1) entitled 'Steps to Success'; it is devised for you to record your thoughts related to each of the 11 Steps. This then becomes your wellbeing plan of action. The framework I have used within 'Steps to Success' could also be incorporated into your staff meetings at school. Discussing each of the 'Steps to Success' would encourage professional dialogue around teacher wellbeing and could be especially useful if staff wellbeing hasn't been a priority before.

> For example, one of the schools I am affiliated with has a wellbeing notice board in their staff room that was instigated following discussions around Step 10 (I use my Steps within the 'Teacher Wellbeing' workshops I have delivered). All staff contribute to this wellbeing board by adding ideas to it about the ways they support their own wellbeing; staff are then able to magpie any ideas that appeal to them. When I visit this school, I always read the new additions to the board. I am amazed by how regularly the wellbeing board is used, considering how busy the staff are. Sometimes it features positive affirmations or anonymous notes thanking a colleague for their support. It also features business cards, such as one from the local yoga studio, and recipes for healthy, nutritious meals and luxurious, comforting puddings. The Headteacher has commented that it has been very constructive in encouraging staff solidarity and has boosted morale. One teacher has even taken this idea forward with her pupils where they share wellbeing ideas and strategies via a classroom wellbeing board. She claims it has had a positive impact and that many parents have commented on how useful their children find it. Apparently, one boy even advised his mother about her wellbeing by telling her that she may benefit from fresh air and a nice walk in natural surroundings!

Assessing your wellbeing

At the end of Part 1, you are encouraged to complete a wellbeing assessment entitled 'How's my wellbeing?' This will give you a basic idea of how you score in terms of physical, emotional, career, social and community wellbeing.

If you are a school leader and are concerned about a colleague or staff member, I suggest that you start by assessing their wellbeing and finding out how ready, or reluctant, they are to discuss their feelings with you. I imagine the extent to how welcome different staff members may be for you to get involved in their wellbeing will vary. It may be best, if you are particularly worried about a staff member, to merely admit that you are worried and then see how they respond. Perhaps some of your staff would be touched that you cared, whereas others might find this akin to an interrogation, so ideally you should tread carefully. In the Education Support Partnership's 'Teacher Wellbeing Index' (2019), it was found that 54% of educational institutions did not regularly survey their staff to assess for wellbeing levels. This signifies how staff wellbeing assessments could have the potential to initiate positive change in schools. Your staff wellbeing assessments can be revisited and updated so that useful strategies that relate to each area of wellbeing are added with time. You will soon become aware that, just by encouraging discussions around mental health, you are in fact facilitating a constructive first stride towards developing whole-school wellbeing for your staff.

At the end of each chapter, the 'Useful resources' section will help you to work towards any personal targets you set, and the 'Takeaway message' comprises of a closing reflection or a key point to consider to be ready for the next chapter.

Step 1: Check in to your wellbeing and take breaks

This book constantly reinforces the importance of becoming more self-aware regarding your health. It highlights the benefit of regularly 'checking in' to assess your physical, mental and emotional wellbeing during the day. I am a firm believer in the importance of tending to your own needs primarily, before the needs of children in your care; this practice of self-care is selfless, not selfish, as being healthy allows you to look after others more effectively. As primary teachers, you will have 30 small people to consider and help flourish, which is an overwhelming responsibility unless you are, first- and-foremost, mentally and physically in good shape. An example of the type of pressure you may be under during a teaching day is the stress of playground duty when you may have hundreds of children to supervise.

At times like this, your wellbeing is crucial (together with a cup of tea and a wooly hat; why are school playgrounds the coldest places on earth with wind speeds of a 100 miles per hour!?). I urge you to make sure that you have small breaks during the day, especially after playground duty, so you can recharge and warm up. After all, your effectiveness at facilitating learning in the classroom will be diminished if you do not have enough breaks.

> My TA, who was able to provide cover supervision, allowed me to grab about five minutes after my playground duty while she facilitated a quick SPAG session with the class. However, without breaks in the first 15 years of my teaching career, I dreaded playground duty, and this story illustrates another reason why:
>
> In my third year of teaching (in 2000), I mislaid (!) a six-year-old boy. He had decided to start walking home on his own during afternoon playtime. There were close to 180 children on the playground and only two adults (the TA and myself). No gates surrounded the playground (safeguarding was very different in those days!), and so Kyle slipped around the side of one of the buildings without being spotted and escaped. Fortunately, this story ended well; Kyle's mum met him as she walked the same route in the opposite direction on the school-run trip. Thankfully, she immediately brought him back to school to inform us of his safety. I was grateful that she was as relaxed about the incident as she appeared; she laughed and referred to Kyle as a 'cheeky monkey'.
>
> Incidentally, one of the challenges of teaching, and dealing with people, is that it is impossible to predict how an innocent remark may be interpreted. This unpredictability can be a source of stress in itself. For example, in reference to the term 'cheeky monkey', it was reported that a teacher was recently suspended for calling a child a 'cheeky monkey', which, I am guessing, was not meant as the racist slur inferred by the child's parent. With examples like this, it's no wonder our wellbeing as teachers suffer as we continually cope with the increasing responsibility and worry of being misinterpreted.
>
> Similarly, I once translated the French word 'grosse' to a child as 'fat' (as she wasn't sure what 'large' meant) and her mother wrote a letter of complaint to the Headteacher about my inappropriate use of the word. After this, I second-guessed and scrutinized the words that I used in the classroom for fear of being challenged by angry parents. I allowed this incident to affect my wellbeing as I spiraled into daily worries relating to my language usage while teaching. I wish I had remembered that as teachers, we are still only imperfect human beings and can't always behave exactly as others expect. I feel that if we try our best and our intentions are good, then this is what should matter the most.

> *Anyway, back to my story about Kyle now… Despite Kyle's mother's understanding attitude, my wellbeing was in tatters that evening, and I even contemplated leaving teaching to avoid something similar happening again. I blamed myself and questioned my teaching ability. This feeling remained with me over the years and affected my confidence. Although, I now realise that my responsibility as a class teacher should not have stretched to keeping the school grounds secure. I would, however, highlight the importance of trying not to lose any children from your school playground!*
>
> *Generally, if you can get to the end of the day without making the same mistakes that I have over the last 20 years, please feel free to celebrate! I am, however, going to forgive myself now for those mistakes and 'let go', because that's the path to wellbeing right there! I am going to try to recall the things that have gone well in my career and hopefully share some of those with you too throughout my writing. However, my own experiences and life circumstances have been particularly traumatic, so I will drip-feed these to you throughout the book rather than pouring my heart out to you on the initial pages.*

Takeaway message: Does the culture of a school shape its staff wellbeing?

The vital thing underpinning and shaping positive teacher wellbeing is the presence of an open and accepting school culture around mental health and staff wellbeing. This would particularly be the existence of an atmosphere that promotes conversations about teacher wellbeing. A teacher could look after all aspects of their physical and mental wellbeing however, this may not be enough if the school culture is not open to teachers engaging in healthy discussions around wellbeing.

Ask yourself—do you think that the organizational culture of your school has a negative effect on your mental health and wellbeing? Forty-nine percent of educational professionals in the Education Support Partnership's 'Teacher Wellbeing Index' (2019) said that they did. This was a new question for the 2019 Teacher Wellbeing Index due to new research-based evidence on the impact of school culture on wellbeing.

Chapter 1 begins by looking at the rationale behind this book and explores the reasons why you may wish to maintain a spotlight on your wellbeing as a teacher…

PART 1

UNDERSTANDING WELLBEING

1

WHY SHOULD TEACHERS SUPPORT THEIR MENTAL HEALTH AND WELLBEING?

What is mental health and wellbeing?

We all have mental health in the same way that we have physical health. The state of our mental health can be influenced by a variety of factors such as relationship issues, stress in the workplace or a combination of 'home' and 'work' circumstances.

It's clear that a person's mental health and wellbeing has a profound impact on their success in work, study and life. The World Health Organisation (WHO) (2005:47) defines mental health as:

> A state of wellbeing in which every individual realises his or her own potential, can cope with the normal stresses of life, can work productively and fruitfully, and is able to make a contribution to her or his community.

The term 'wellbeing' is slightly more generic and problematic to define but can be viewed as incorporating both physical and mental health. Wellbeing is defined in the Oxford English Dictionary as:

The state of being comfortable, healthy or happy.

There are many definitions of teacher wellbeing; one such example from Bending, cited in Luke & Gourd (2018:115), is 'an overall satisfaction in life and current role/position,' relating to one's 'sense of autonomy, control, competence, connectedness and congruence.' Galton & MacBeath (2008) believe that teachers sadly have lost their autonomy and are no longer in control of how and what they teach. This loss of freedom perhaps highlights why so many teachers are struggling with their wellbeing at work. Despite these definitions, your own wellbeing should be approached in unique ways according to what wellbeing means to you, particularly because there is no 'one-size-fits-all' solution to supporting a person's mental health and wellbeing.

Step 2: Previous wellbeing strategies

As you read, it is worth reflecting upon individual strategies in the past that have made you feel relaxed or brought about a sense of balance or wellness in you. This is a good place to start to ensure that you are supporting your wellbeing in ways that resonate with your own personality, values and preferences.

Can wellbeing be measured?

The level of wellbeing in an individual can be difficult to measure. Nevertheless, I encourage you to gauge where your wellbeing currently is by completing the assessment, 'How's my wellbeing?' (at the end of Chapter 2). However, the results will be far from definitive and will provide merely a snapshot of your general wellbeing (which is always subject to change). For this assessment, I use the following categories of wellbeing: physical, emotional, career, social and community.

Other studies that have attempted to measure wellbeing have done so in contrasting ways.

Thorley's report (2017:9) highlights that wellbeing can be 'measured across four key indicators:

- happiness,
- life satisfaction,

- feeling things in life are worthwhile,
- low anxiety.'

In contrast, the Department for Education (DfE) (2019) utilised a different structure for wellbeing within their Teacher Wellbeing Research Report, which listed the main elements of wellbeing as:

- health (how we feel physically and mentally)
- relationships with others at work
- purpose (including clarity of goals, motivation, workload and ability to influence decisions)
- environment (work culture, facilities and tools)
- security (financial security, safety and bullying/harassment)

How does work impact your wellbeing?

Work is significant in making, or breaking, our mental health and wellbeing. WHO (2014) estimated that we spend a third of our adult life at work, thereby suggesting that work constitutes a substantial part of what makes us who we are. Unfortunately, stress at work can aggravate potential mental health issues within us. However, schools with a priority on wellbeing, along with empathetic and well-trained line managers, can play a powerful role in promoting wellbeing and sustaining our good mental health.

Mental Health First Aid England (2016:9) discuss the impact of work on us by purporting that:

> Not only does work give us the money we need to live, but it also provides social contacts and support, keeps us physically and mentally active, allows us to develop and use skills, gives us social status, a sense of identity and personal achievement, and provides a way for us to structure and occupy our time.

Despite the influence of work on our wellbeing, mental ill health can be attributed to non-work factors too. For instance, a teacher experiencing a bereavement or a relationship breakdown who previously found their workload eminently manageable may temporarily be unable to cope at work. If the workplace is not supportive, this can trigger or exacerbate mental ill health and contribute to stress-related disorders, such as anxiety and depression.

Are many teachers feeling the pressure?

Let us turn to statistics and research now, for those of you who like numbers and percentages. Here's an optimistic start and a reason to continue reading this book: It has been found that if wellbeing is addressed in workplaces, productivity is increased by 12% (Oswald et al., 2015). More of a 'doom and gloom' picture is painted from the findings of recent studies about the state of teacher wellbeing…

Kell (2018) found in her survey of 3684 school staff that:

- 66% said they often felt tearful at work
- 54% said their depression was related to their job
- 82% said anxiety was directly related to their job
- 52% said they would strongly disagree with the statement 'my workload is manageable'
- 58% would not recommend teaching to a close friend or relative
- 83% said that they had considered leaving the teaching profession

Teachers in management roles also found the demands overwhelming. Kell discovered that 35% of school leaders admitted to working more than 20 hours per week above their contracted hours and that 73% experienced job-related anxiety.

Fifty-six percent of her sample of all teachers said that they had experienced verbal abuse from a pupil but that this was not the reason they attributed to wanting to leave teaching. It seems that the stress that goes with supporting behavioural problems in the classroom is something that teachers, in her study, understand and accept. However, this acceptance came with the caveat that support is available for them if they experience challenges with pupil behaviour.

Kell found that the top six reasons for people leaving teaching were (starting with the most significant factor):

1) Unreasonable working hours
2) Ofsted (Office for Standards in Education, Children's Services and Skills)

3) Poor mental health related to the job
4) Neglect of other responsibilities, e.g. family, friends, hobbies etc.
5) Negative relationships with colleagues
6) Pupil behaviour

Nevertheless, 88% of Kell's sample concluded that they liked teaching. This indicates that the nature of the job is overtly enjoyable for many teachers but that the pressures that overlie this nature are ruining the job overall.

The Education Support Partnership (ESP) is the UK's only charity providing mental health and wellbeing support services to all educational staff, such as a telephone support helpline (see Useful resources). ESP counsellors have found a significant increase in calls, for example, from 2017 to 2018, with the number of teachers seeking support increasing by 35%. Indeed, the ESP report in the Teacher Wellbeing Index (2019), surveying approximately 3000 educational professionals, indicated that work-related stress had increased for the third consecutive year. The following statistics were recorded (figures relate to all educational professionals, unless otherwise stated):

- 72% described themselves as stressed (84% of school leaders). This is a rise from 67% in 2018, and for school leaders, a rise from 80% in 2018.
- 78% experienced behavioural, psychological or physical symptoms due to their work.
- 71% cited workload as the main reason they consider leaving their jobs.

However, Professor Glazzard's small-scale research (2019), where he interviewed 64 teachers, found that workload was *not* cited as the main issue for leaving a teaching job. Glazzard's sample explained that teachers knew from the outset that the workload involved in their teaching role would be intense. Glazzard found that the biggest issue for his participants was a negative school culture and a toxic environment. Teachers described the feeling of not being trusted, having no autonomy and constantly being held to account. They complained about having no agency and that they were unable to make their own decisions. This indicates that the limelight needs to be on school culture because the wellbeing of a teacher is likely to plummet if they are in a school with a toxic atmosphere and an intolerance for discussions around wellbeing.

Moreover, a worrying statistic uncovered by the Office of National Statistics (2017) showed that between 2011 and 2015, suicide rates among nursery and primary school teachers in England was nearly double the national average.

> One of my closest friends, an excellent classroom practitioner of 15 years, has recently left the teaching profession due to the relentless pressure placed upon her. Her last visit from Ofsted was the final straw. Prior to and during this inspection, she witnessed and experienced unbearable tension and disappointment as she failed to perform as she had hoped under the watchful and stern eyes of Her Majesty's Inspectors (HMI). She had always worked to a high standard in the classroom, but faced with the pressure of being observed constantly, she crumbled. Her school had insisted on many observations leading up to the Ofsted visit, which left her feeling drained and demotivated. She also felt as if she was letting down her entire school by struggling with her observation nerves. It was all too much. After a visit to her doctor who prescribed her with anti-depressants, she spent a month at home recuperating. Once she felt better, she had a hard think about what was next for her, and the thought of returning to the same pressures and stresses were impossible for her to contemplate. She is now relishing in the new-found joys of working as a postal worker. She admitted that since exiting from teaching, she has regained her spark and appreciation for life that had been buried under vast amounts of previous worry associated with her teaching role.
>
> I went through a period of my life where I struggled to cope with the demands of working as a teacher and, in addition, trying to fulfil my role as a mother to six-month-old twins and a two-year-old daughter. Having returned from a short maternity leave, I was unable to go back into the year group I felt comfortable teaching in and was told that I needed to cover the Planning, Preparation and Assessment (PPA) time for a Year 6 class (which had a variety of children with severe special needs in it). I recall finishing the days in Year 6 feeling absolutely strung out with my nerves in shreds. I have a faint memory of crying as I walked home every night, which seemed the only way to release the pent-up anxiety that had been bubbling up inside me all day while teaching. I was desperate to hide my true feelings of dread about returning to work from my family, so I knew that the walk home was the only time I had to let out my sadness. My main struggles were dealing with about 10 boisterous pupils in the Year 6 class and attempting to control their behaviour. In addition, I was struggling with maths subject knowledge due to my

jump from a Year 1 to Year 6 class. If my family life hadn't been so hectic, then I could have spent time researching the methods of teaching algebra, etc., so that I could have felt more confident about my lessons. However, with three children under three years of age, it was impossible for me to spend the time at home I needed to prepare properly.

Then, my best friend died from a brain tumour just when I thought she was getting better. This news culminated in me finding that I could no longer function in my capacity as mum and teacher; the demands from children in all areas of my life became utterly overwhelming and I felt I was doing everything wrong. With my first daughter, I had been able to read her a bedtime story every night for the first year of her life, but with my twins first birthday soon approaching, it suddenly dawned on me that I had rarely spent any time reading to them. I was barely surviving and just existing moment to moment, constantly feeding, changing nappies and then working at school in an environment completely out of my comfort zone. I suspect that I was experiencing the side effects of sleep deprivation and exhaustion. This resulted in me not being able to get out of bed one day and crying uncontrollably. When I finally visited the doctor, she diagnosed me with postnatal depression. Furthermore, I was in shock following my best friend's death and consumed with feelings of guilt that I hadn't been a good enough friend to her. I had forgotten my own wellbeing in an attempt to carry on day after day with the determination to not let a single person know how badly I was feeling.

There is no shame in admitting that you aren't coping; I wish now that I had spoken to someone sooner. This story isn't all negative, as I will share with you a few strategies that helped me to build myself up to returning to work (in Part 2). One of these strategies, alas, involved me retraining in an area outside of education though (massage and beauty therapy), so that I could earn money and thereby decrease my teaching hours in school; it did offer me a passion for something that was not teaching- or child-related. When my health improved, I returned to full-time teaching, though. It is a sad state of affairs if support is not available now to teachers feeling the same way as I did 15 years ago. If help did exist then, I wasn't aware of it.

Surely we need to work at keeping teachers in the job. Feeling stressed is often due to the fact that teachers care so much about children; they sometimes work themselves into the ground for the sake of pupils. This book will outline many ideas for a teacher to try before ultimately making the decision to leave teaching behind. However, perhaps teaching is not for everyone. If your wellbeing is suffering due to the job pressures and you have exhausted all options and avenues to address this, it is understandable that you would want to try an alternative career path.

> *Another of my close friends taught for a total of 18 years before she decided to drop back on the pressure at work. This move was instigated by her divorce and a change of perspective. She worked in the mornings as a teaching assistant and in the evenings as an English and maths tutor. She relished the chance to work with children in a more relaxed capacity. However, after two years in these roles, she decided to search for a full-time teaching post once more. She is feeling positive that she is in a much better place now to cope with the accountability and associated workload of teaching.*

Supporting your own wellbeing as a teacher

A teacher contends with a torrent of demands and pressures each day; many hats are placed daily upon teachers' heads, such as educator, nurse, counsellor, sports instructor and more. It has been implied that a teacher makes over 1500 educational decisions every school day, which is:

> …a constant juggle of manager, content holder, master communicator, and support system, (TeachThought Staff, 2016a, 2016b).

Therefore, it is understandable that so many teachers feel overwhelmed. In support of this, Dr Boogren (2018:1) claims that:

> Teachers make more minute by minute decisions than brain surgeons.

She explains that having to multitask is the reason why many teachers are exhausted. Boogren's book (2018), which is structured using Maslow's Hierarchy of Needs (1943), emphasises the importance of teachers looking after themselves; this mirrors my own views.

Establishing regular opportunities for self-care is vital to protect your wellbeing. In many ways, teaching is like acting; you are performing in a variety of roles to an audience. You won't always feel like playing your part, but you have no choice, and sometimes you may feel like you are under intense scrutiny. The sad fact is that often the more that you give to your job, the more that will be expected of you. Therefore, you need to be realistic about what you can and cannot manage to give to your work after considering the other roles you need to fulfil, such as parent, spouse, sibling or carer.

Step 3: Learn to say 'no'

Often, a clever move for teachers under pressure is to learn to say 'no' occasionally and be selective about what you commit to.

> Writing this feels uncomfortable for me, as I've never been able to say 'no' easily. It's a 'pot calling the kettle black' moment, but as I am learning, the older (and wiser, hopefully) I get.
>
> In my younger teaching days (when my wrinkles were much less noticeable than they are now), I was so desperate to create a good impression that saying 'no' was a very alien concept for me. I am a self-confessed 'people pleaser', which means that I allow myself to get manipulated into doing a bombardment of extra things at work. I do this so that I am viewed as helpful and am well-liked at work. I enjoy working in a team collaboratively, which gives me job satisfaction but means that I take on a lot more than I should (especially if I want to reduce my stress, which is obviously detrimental to my wellbeing). Frequently, I emerge from meetings with a long list of actions that I had agreed to complete so that I could attempt to maintain my persona as a team player.
>
> The story that follows is an example of me not being brave enough to say 'no':
>
> During my job interview for the second teaching job of my career, I boasted that I had been on a rugby training course whilst studying for my B.Ed (Hons) degree. What I didn't explain was that the training had only been for half a day, and for most of it, I had been nursing a hangover, so hadn't, in fact, taken on board much of the content.
>
> That night, after the job interview, I was offered the job and I accepted.
>
> On my first visit day (in July, before I was due to start as a Reception class teacher in September), the Headteacher congratulated me and announced that the reason for my appointment, above all the other candidates, was my expertise in football! Not wanting to appear stupid, I grinned and nodded while internally freaking out and wondering what he meant by 'expertise', and in 'football'!? The conversation went drastically downhill then, as the Headteacher proudly offered me the position of after-school football coach to Key Stage 2 boys. What else could I have done but graciously accept with a fake smile (grimace) and a delighted giggle (nervous laugh)? I know now that I should have

explained that I was not qualified in the least for this position and was very far from a 'football expert'. What I should have said, so as not to appear rude, was that perhaps I could offer my services to a different after-school club, like yoga or dance, that was more suitable to my skill set. But I didn't.

What then transpired was that my summer before starting that post was taken over by copious amounts of holiday reading. It wasn't my usual holiday reading (chick-flick novels and magazines) but books about football and how to coach it. I started in the children's section of the local library by reading 10 nonfiction books entitled 'How to play football'. Six weeks later, I still hadn't a clue what the offside rule entailed, despite my partner explaining it to me about a hundred times!

As you can probably guess, being a football coach was sheer hell for me, and (need I say?) it affected my wellbeing in the first few months of starting my new job. I dreaded it every Wednesday at 3.15pm. The boys could tell that I was clueless about football just from the language I used and my very poor dribbling skills when I demonstrated a task. My role as football coach was made worse by an unpopular decision I made. I wished to encourage fair play and provide an opportunity for all the boys who attended the football club to play against the local teams in the league. Therefore, I changed the squad so that everyone had the chance to play. I really believed that it was the right thing to do—it's the 'taking part' that's the important bit, not the winning, surely? I hadn't counted on the competitiveness of 10-year-old boys! Or their dads! I got verbal abuse from the fathers that stood on the sidelines during every football match. They shouted at me when I substituted a player or refused to argue at the referee. The trouble was, I barely knew what was going on (on the pitch), so I stayed quiet most of the time apart from feebly shouting, 'Score a goal!'

Needless to say, we didn't win the league that year (like we had the previous year—to add insult to injury!). My saving grace was a young, newly appointed teacher who joined the school and began helping me on a Wednesday with football club. Eventually I phased myself out of being the coach as he took more and more responsibility—after all, he was desperate to look good. Thank goodness he was a 'people pleaser', too!

Supporting the wellbeing of your staff

A happy and healthy school is only possible if teachers' wellbeing is ranked highly by school leaders and considered as important as pupil wellbeing. Ideally, managers need to be either naturally skilled at spotting early signs of mental ill health or trained to recognise and identify poor wellbeing in their staff. In the most basic of terms, a manager is most effective if they are comfortable talking about wellbeing and can direct their staff to available wellbeing resources. This can create a climate where teachers are trusting of school leaders and feel confident to talk openly about any mental health or wellbeing problems they are experiencing. The best way to break down existing stigma and discrimination around mental health problems is to talk more openly and honestly about your feelings and emotions. Stigma can be perceived as a major obstacle that prevents teachers from talking to senior staff about their problems, regardless of how open a manager may be. Some teachers may fear discrimination or feel shameful of their mental health needs. Moreover, thoughts of stigma may prevent teachers from acknowledging their feelings, even to themselves.

If school leaders support the mental health of their staff effectively in a timely and empathic way, then teachers are much more likely to stay in the teaching profession. Supporting and nurturing early-career teachers has been found to be particularly essential due to evidence of their struggles. For example, an Association of Teachers and Lecturers (ATL) survey (2015) found that 73% of trainee and newly qualified teachers considered leaving the profession; 76% of these blamed heavy workloads as the main factor for this (Exley, 2015; Hodge, 2015). Newland (who I met on two occasions when he visited my university) was quoted in an article as saying:

> There is too much demanded—often on pain of failure or censure—on young teachers who are still learning the craft. They should be allowed time and tolerance to think creatively, make mistakes and learn from them (Hodge, 2015).

Keates, secretary of the National Association of Schoolmasters and Union of Women Teachers.(NASUWT), said:

> Too many employers are failing to exercise their duty of care… The time has come to end the culture of the 'anything goes' style of management where any adverse impact on teachers is regarded as collateral damage (Santry, 2018).

Many school leaders do know, however, that the best way to increase productivity is not to pile on the pressure, but to engage staff and listen to their concerns. However, it is fair to say that a certain amount of pressure may help to motivate staff and boost their energy levels and dedication, especially if there are rewards available. It is worth remembering that staff can feel stressed when too *few* demands are made on them, for instance when they are bored or under-stimulated.

A staff member who is at work but struggling daily with their mental health can be referred to as a 'presentee'; they are merely going through the motions of their job despite having low wellbeing. You may recognise this in a colleague when you ask if they are okay and they answer 'fine', but their eyes and demeanour tell another story. Unless action is taken to support this person, then it is very likely that they will develop into an 'absentee' who may need a long period of absence to deal with the effects of being at work for so long whilst experiencing ill health. You can learn to observe the signs of 'presentee-ism' in staff. I list the signs of stress and burnout in Chapter 2; having this knowledge will allow you to pre-empt avoidable absence and offer support at the earliest stage. As a school leader, you are not necessarily expected to be an expert on mental health and wellbeing, but it helps if you are informed about a few basic ways to support staff that need a little extra help to remain happy and healthy at work. Ideas can be as simple as sticking posters on the inside of toilet doors advertising the Education Support Partnership and the helpline number (see Useful resources).

The mental health and wellbeing of school leaders

Due to the accountable nature of being a school leader, there is bound to be pressure on you from many angles. In Chapter 5, I list the possible support available for school leaders. In dealing with your own stress, you need to be vigilant about not transferring it to your staff. It is crucial for school leaders to model how they support their own personal wellbeing, such as by maintaining perspective, a sense of humour and a positive work-life balance. This modelling is imperative for early-career teachers to witness so that they can be guided to have a focus on wellbeing in the initial stages of their careers.

If you are feeling the pressure, then ask for help if appropriate and you feel able to. Consider sharing your feelings of being overwhelmed with other colleagues, as this may encourage teamwork and cooperation. Often staff members will feel honoured that you need them and be grateful for your honesty in sharing your own foibles. Having said that, struggling with one's wellbeing should never be viewed as a weakness.

If you are comfortable enough to share your lived experience of mental health struggles, or those of a person close to you, then this can be a very powerful way to normalize mental health matters at work. I discuss the value and benefit of this in Chapter 5. However, sharing your own personal circumstances should not be forced, and you should only ever share what you feel comfortable divulging. By talking about mental health in a non-judgmental way, this will demonstrate that you have an accepting attitude towards those staff that have mental health troubles. This may ultimately lead to a staff member feeling able to discuss their mental health with you. Subsequently, you are given a chance to address their needs rather than allowing their mental health to deteriorate.

Government guidance and perspectives

Let us consider the wider context and national picture for a moment and what the government's perspectives may entail. The DfE accept that data management can create unnecessary workloads for teachers. Hinds (2018), the Secretary of State for Education, acknowledges that teachers are 'overwhelmed by excessive workloads' and 'drowning in meaningless data', and that there is no easy answer to easing workloads. Hinds admits that teachers work excessively long hours and unveiled plans to improve teacher recruitment to attract more teachers to the profession (Whittaker, 2019). Hinds' recruitment plans include a new two-year training package for new teachers, a reduced timetable, and rewards and bonuses. He promises an investment of £130 million will be devoted to teacher recruitment each year. Hinds specifies that the new workload toolkit from the DfE would help, as it would highlight how schools have minimised onerous practices and policies for others to learn from (Adams & Stewart, 2018).

Labour's Shadow Education Secretary, Rayner, comments on Mr Hinds' remarks, saying:

> The best thing the Government could do for teachers' morale is commit to new funding to give our teachers the pay they deserve (Independent, 2018).

This indicates that the reason for the disillusionment of teachers is due to heavy workloads and poor pay and conditions, as already indicated by a plethora of findings and research.

Keates highlights:

> '...a crisis in teacher supply' and blamed 'increasing teacher workloads, dwindling pay, uncompetitive starting salaries... and the relentless pressure' (Speck, 2019).

The DfE (2019a:11) confirm that retention of teachers has been a challenge, especially among early-career teachers. For example, over 20% of new teachers left the profession within their first two years of teaching, and 33% within their first five years.

Moran, Liberal Democrat MP, warns that 'Government ministers would do well to take heed' of the immense pressure placed upon teachers, which could potentially lead to burnout. She comments:

> As a former teacher, I know how hard teachers work to give young people the best chance in life. They must never be left vulnerable to mental ill-health, particularly because of a failed system of mishandled inspections or a culture of ill-judged high-stakes testing. (Kitchen, 2018).

The changing role of a teacher

It has been apparent that over the last 20 years, the job of a teacher has changed significantly and, maybe for some, has taken the joy out of the role. Galton & MacBeath (2008:4–5) support this thinking and specify that:

> successive government reforms have succeeded in progressively draining off the enthusiasm and commitment for teaching, so that the greatest professional source of satisfaction—seeing children learn—is progressively undermined by tables, targets and the tyranny of testing.

Ofsted (2019a:4) report that teachers:

> ...do not have enough influence over policy, which changes too quickly.

The negative impact of changing policy increases the already high workload, and the perceived lack of control and autonomy leads to feelings of 'de-professionalisation'.

Suggestions for this rise in bureaucracy and teacher pressure in the UK is related to a drop in the number of Ofsted inspectors, meaning that schools are under increasing pressure to collect information during inspection. Moreover, since 2010, penalties have been more severe for schools if an inspection has not gone well, resulting in the consequential demotivation of teaching staff.

Galton & MacBeath (2008:5) explain that:

> '…classrooms are now more transparent, and the nature of teaching and learning are open to almost continuous scrutiny' which is clear could lead to increased stress and pressure placed on our teachers.

It seems that schools were morphing into exam factories where the focus was mainly on their data. However, with the new Education Inspection Framework (2019) I am hopeful that this may be set to change, with a promise of more focus on curriculum rather than results.

The consequences of testing

If teachers are overly worried about results, then this is often reflected by the weight given to Statutory Assessment Tests (SATs) within a school. When Spielman (Chief Inspector for Ofsted) presented the new Ofsted Education Inspection Framework (EIF) (2019b), she highlighted in a BBC News article (Burns, 2019) that schools should avoid unintentionally intensifying the importance of Year 6 SATs. One may argue that the exam stress of SATs could develop resilience and prepare children for the real world and their up-and-coming General Certificate of Secondary Education (GCSEs). However, I cannot see how exposing children to exam stress can ever be a good thing.

Having read an inspiring Times Educational Supplement (TES) article by clinical psychologist Dr Porter (2019), I have reflected upon the impact of SATs in a school both from the perspective of a child and a teacher. It is clear that within a school, anxiety can be easily transmittable and if great significance is put on tests, then this can add to a climate of worry for both staff and pupils. The overwhelming effect of this stress could leave children feeling that they are unworthy if they do not perform according to the school's high expectations, and this can be paralleled with teachers feeling unworthy, too.

Optimistically, Ofsted's new EIF (2019c) does appear to have pupil's and teacher's workloads in mind, but the impact of this new way of inspecting schools has yet to be fully evaluated in practice. A report from the Association of School and College Leaders (ASCL) (2020) appears in the Useful resources for this chapter, if you wish to read about their survey's findings. As a little taster, when participants were asked, 'Are you satisfied that the current inspection system consistently, fairly and accurately judges the performance of schools and colleges?', it was shown that 88.52% answered 'no'. However, to provide a balanced view, Ofsted (2020) found the reverse from conducting a post-inspection survey; 88.6% of their respondents were satisfied with inspections in their state-funded school (also in Useful resources).

The new Ofsted Education Inspection Framework (EIF)

With the changes to the Ofsted EIF, it has been implied that there will be a focus on teacher workload whereby schools will be encouraged not to use data collection

> in a way that creates unnecessary burdens for staff or learners
>
> (2019a:13).

The new framework encourages leaders to recognise any workload pressures upon staff and deal with these quickly and appropriately. Staff wellbeing is a key feature, and judgement will be made within the leadership and management section of the framework. It appears that inspectors will be assessing whether there is a focus on excessive, unnecessary internal data within a school; school leaders will be asked to explain their rationale related to this, as there are so many factors that affect a school's outcomes that are beyond a Headteacher's control. Indeed, the criteria for outstanding leadership includes the statement:

> Staff consistently report high levels of support for well-being issues.

The impact on teacher wellbeing remains to be seen from changes made to the EIF. There appear to be a few schools appealing against their recent Ofsted gradings. One article reported that children were questioned so intensively by Ofsted inspectors that a few were in tears. An Ofsted spokesperson said:

> our new inspections are unapologetically not just about grades- we are looking at the overall quality of education…this approach recognises strong approaches to the curriculum, good leadership and a real determination to do the best for all pupils (Lightfoot, 2020).

On a more positive note, the consultation involved in the changes to the framework included the mental health charity Young Minds. This demonstrates that the DfE and officials are aware of the disastrous effects of neglecting pupil wellbeing. Moreover, when one links to the potential negative impact on children who may be being taught by teachers that experience low wellbeing, the need to change the system as it stands becomes even more urgent.

The impact of teacher wellbeing on pupil progress

Let's explore now, using a more positive slant, how a teacher with very good wellbeing could impact the children they teach. I am aware my writing so far may have stressed the poor wellbeing of teachers and omitted to acknowledge that there are many teachers thriving contentedly and experiencing high levels of wellbeing within the job parameters and all that teaching entails. The ESP's Teacher Wellbeing Index (2019:22) found that the top reasons for job satisfaction among educational professionals were:

- Making a difference/impact
- Helping young people achieve their potential
- Interaction with students
- Every day is different

In short, research indicates, as you would probably expect, that good teacher wellbeing has a beneficial effect on children's learning. In 2007, the first UK study of its kind was conducted that found that teacher wellbeing was indeed linked to pupil performance. The research was undertaken by

Professor Briner & Dr Dewberry in partnership with Worklife Support. They looked at the correlation between teacher wellbeing and SAT data over the core subjects.

The research was underpinned by the view that if a teacher experiences a high level of job satisfaction, then they will operate more effectively in their teaching role, and therefore, this will instigate a positive impact on pupil progress. Wellbeing was measured using an online survey and looked at wellbeing in relation to three factors:

- Feeling valued and cared for
- Feeling overloaded
- Job stimulation and enjoyment

Data was gathered from 24,100 staff in 246 primary schools and 182 high schools, but the focus was on primary schools when data was analysed. One of the key findings was that 92% of the variation in SAT scores were related to other factors and 8% was accounted for by teacher wellbeing. Although this figure of 8% appears relatively insignificant, the researchers explain that, in fact:

> ...it is statistically significant and may be practically important because teacher wellbeing may be more amenable to intervention and change than other factors known to strongly affect SATs scores (such as social class).

It is important also to establish that if pupils perform well, then this may inadvertently affect teacher wellbeing in a positive way, rather than the other way around. In other words, just as it has been found that increases in teacher wellbeing can lead to better pupil performance, likewise increases in pupil performance may lead to increased wellbeing in teachers.

Briner & Dewberry (2007:4) indicate that the relationship between teacher wellbeing and pupil performance is subject to both 'virtuous circles and downward spirals' according to how happy teachers feel within their jobs. The conclusions from this study state that if we want to improve a school's performance, then a tight focus needs to be on teacher wellbeing. Briner & Dewberry (2007:4) suggest:

Happier motivated teachers may make pupils feel happier, motivated and more confident.

Bajorek et al. (2014) built on the Briner and Dewberry's research and show that when a teacher promotes pupil wellbeing, academic outcomes improve. Consequently, if a teacher makes supporting the mental wellbeing of their class a priority, then they are more likely to support their own wellbeing. The authors assert that in this current climate, it is crucial that schools 'make the most of their key resource—teachers'. Bajorek et al. conclude that the education sector needs to improve their ability to understand teacher wellbeing by monitoring teacher absence, especially from mental ill health. They suggest that the education sector should learn from the strong links that the National Health Service (NHS) have reported; research undertaken in the NHS found that when staff health and wellbeing is good, then good patient outcomes have been observed, and vice versa (Boorman Review, 2009).

It has been found that the productivity of a teacher drastically reduces when they attend work when unwell. In the ESP's Teacher Wellbeing Index (2019), 49% of educational professionals said that they felt compelled to attend school when they were unwell, which shows how common this is and the strong potential for children to be affected.

However, when teachers are absent from work due to low wellbeing, it has been uncovered that there are negative impacts upon pupil learning and behaviour (Estyn, 2013) and pupil wellbeing (Harding et al., 2019). Teacher absenteeism is a growing problem; the Department for Education (2012) found that 55% of teachers had at least one stint of absence a year due to sickness. The Estyn Report highlights how teacher absence results in poorer-quality lessons, especially when children are taught by supply teachers who often do not know pupils well enough to appropriately address their learning or pastoral needs.

Glazzard (2018) in association with Teachwire.net, surveyed 770 teachers and found that:

- 77% thought their poor mental health was having a detrimental effect on the progress of their pupils
- 89% admitted that their mental health had a negative impact on the creativity of their lessons

- 85% thought their mental health problems were likely to decrease the quality of their lesson planning
- 81% agreed or strongly agreed that their poor mental health negatively impacted the quality of their relationships with pupils

In support of this, Harding et al. (2019) found an association between good teacher wellbeing and lower pupil psychological issues, and lower teacher depression and good pupil wellbeing.

A year later, Glazzard (2019) interviewed teachers from 10 primary schools with both good and poor mental health and found that their teacher wellbeing was affected by:

- pressure during busy times of year
- extracurricular activities they have to deliver
- keeping up with changes, especially changes in school leadership
- difficulties in their personal lives

He asked what strategies they had to cope with poor wellbeing, and they cited:

- exercise
- meditation
- being organised
- ensuring that they had time for hobbies and family
- coming to terms and making peace with the fact that jobs were rarely accomplished
- having the realisation that it's impossible to do everything perfectly (I discuss the issue of the perfectionist tendency of teachers in Chapter 4)

Useful resources

- The Useful Resources sections of this book can be accessed with one click via my website: www.supportingteacherwellbeing.wordpress.com
- The Health and Safety Executive Management Standards (2017) report some advice for managers and employees regarding how to deal with common mental health problems at work. This will be discussed in more detail in Part 2, but this webpage is worth reading, especially as there is a free Tackling Stress workbook that you may find useful: http://www.hse.gov.uk/stress/mental-health.htm

- The Education Support Partnership (ESP) offers help and support for anyone working in education.
  Phone: 0800 0562 561 (Freephone, 24 hours a day, 7 days a week)
  Text: 07903 341229
  Email: support@edsupport.org.uk
  Website: www.educationsupportpartnership.org.uk/chat-support
- The 'Teach Thought: We grow teachers' website found at: https://www.teachthought.com/ provides resources and learning tools for teachers.
- You can find the ASCL survey here: https://www.ascl.org.uk/News/Our-news-and-press-releases/School-leaders-say-Ofsted-requires-improvement
- Ofsted's results from post-inspection surveys can be found here: https://www.gov.uk/government/publications/responses-to-post-inspection-surveys-state-funded-schools

Takeaway message: Do pupils notice low wellbeing in teachers?

Glazzard (2019) interviewed 64 pupils in 10 primary schools and found that children can pick up on when their teacher is experiencing low wellbeing. This exposes the idea of an 'emotional contagion' where our feelings and moods as a teacher may be contagious to children. He found that the facial expressions of teachers were a signal to children of how their teacher was feeling, and that pupils noticed the times when teachers were struggling. The children he interviewed described their teachers as often being 'frustrated' and 'stressed'. These children admitted to regulating their behaviour and deliberately getting on quietly with their work due to 'an obligation not to make things worse' (2019:5); for example, during times when their teacher's wellbeing was off-kilter.

Again, research such as this has strongly validated the need for a tight focus on improving teacher wellbeing. This book gives you the knowledge, strategies and practical assistance to support wellbeing at an individual and school-wide level. Let me share now, in the next chapter, some knowledge surrounding mental health and wellbeing so that you are forearmed with the necessary information that you can apply to your practices and attitudes as a teacher.

2

WHAT DO YOU NEED TO KNOW ABOUT WELLBEING?

A mental health continuum for teachers

It is normal and natural to have highs and lows in your mental health, and this ever-changing movement from one state to another can be illustrated by the mental health continuum model below (Figure 2.1).

The arrows on this model suggest movement in both directions along a continuum, indicating that there is always the possibility for a return to full health and functioning. It is important to understand that a person diagnosed with a mental illness can still have high levels of general mental wellbeing, and conversely, a person without a diagnosed mental illness can show low levels of mental wellbeing. Even over small periods of time, your mood will change and thus your mental health will vary, often in response to your thoughts and whether they are positive or negative. The 'check-in' (see Step 1) that you complete during your teaching days will allow you to assess where you are in each moment. You can use the mental health continuum model as a benchmark to help gauge your own, or someone else's, state of mind. It is vital to remember that anyone can develop mental ill

WHAT DO YOU NEED TO KNOW ABOUT WELLBEING? 33

Mentally healthy teacher	Teacher with emerging mental health needs	Teacher with advanced mental health concerns	Teacher with severe mental health issues
Healthy	Emerging	Advanced	Severe
Normal changes in mood Consistent sleep patterns Good energy levels No physical ailments Socially active Performs well in class Happy and thriving in school	Slightly irritable, nervous teacher Some difficulty sleeping Often tired with low energy levels Muscle tension and headaches Decreased social activity Some performance inconsistencies Sometimes unhappy at school	Anxious, angry and frustrated teacher Sleep disturbances are common Tiredness and fatigue Aches and pains Social withdrawal or avoidance Decreased performance ('presentee-ism') Feelings of hopelessness and sadness	Teacher with excessive anxiety Unable to sleep or stay asleep Exhaustion and burn-out Extreme tiredness Social isolation Unable to perform ('absentee-ism') Severe depression and pervasive sadness
Actions that a teacher can take at each stage of the continuum – further details in Part 2 of *Supporting Teacher Wellbeing*			
Carry on as you are Continue to focus on self-care Separate jobs into manageable chunks Relaxation strategies when needed Continue to use support networks Help others in school with wellbeing Continue with healthy lifestyle	Become more self-aware to your dips Recognise your limits Identify and minimise your stressors Get adequate rest Practice mindfulness Focus on healthy eating and exercise Share with a trusted colleague Tell a senior manager about your dip Contact the Education Support Partnership (ESP) GP visit	Identify when you are distressed Alert a senior manager and share Seek social support from colleagues Consider professional support Visit your GP for guidance Contact the ESP for advice	Urgently seek professional help Rest! Keep in touch with support networks Keep in touch with senior staff Take a holiday or break if you are able

Figure 2.1 Allies' Mental health continuum for teachers model.

health at any time in their life, just as they can a physical illness. Poor mental health can be triggered by a range of circumstances and affects different people in a variety of contrasting ways.

You would have reason to be concerned about someone's mental health if you observed a sudden and drastic change from one state to another, or if you notice that a person stays in a low state for a long period of time. In general, we can categorise mental ill health as temporary, fluctuating or ongoing. If the mental health condition is ongoing, then the person experiencing it might control their illness through one, or a combination, of the following: medication (for example, antidepressants or beta-blockers), talking therapies (for example, Cognitive Behavioural Therapy), self-help or practical support. This book will focus on the latter two of these controlling methods. Self-help and practical support both rely on an autonomous approach and can work either alongside medication and talking therapies, or as an initial measure to assess whether you can help yourself or if you need to seek additional support. Part 2 of this book will guide you through the various self-help methods for you to consider, including mindfulness, positive thinking and improving your mood with exercise.

The mental health continuum model mentions the terms 'presentee-ism' and 'absentee-ism' under the 'Advanced' and 'Severe' categories. I have already introduced these terms, so now you can see how this relates to the mental health continuum model: The presentee-ism state is the beginning of a dip in wellbeing where a teacher may feel stressed due to work circumstances or pressure, or it may be caused by non-work factors that are negatively impacting their mental health. This will ultimately have a negative effect on the learners in their class. This state, unless help is available, tends to result in 'absentee-ism', where the teacher receives time off work to regain their wellbeing. Incidentally, the cost of mental health issues in England is estimated at between £16.8-£26.4 billion each year (Deloitte MCS Ltd, 2017).

As teachers, therefore, you need to take responsibility that you are 'fit for purpose', as help and support from outside agencies, or even your school, will not necessarily be forthcoming. You can ensure this by maintaining a healthy body and a healthy mind, resting and sleeping sufficiently and managing your time effectively. You can also develop 'communities of practice' (Smith & McGrandles, 2018) by monitoring and supporting colleagues. This can be achieved by recognising 'presentee-ism' in your colleagues and sharing information on wellbeing with each other. The practicalities of peer support among school colleagues is discussed in Chapter 5. Perhaps buy this book as a gift for one of your colleagues (sorry for that blatant marketing strategy!) to encourage a peer-support system in your school. The work of Rogers (2012), which is mentioned throughout this book, emphasises the usefulness of collegial support for teacher wellbeing.

> In reference to the mental health continuum, my own mental health dropped one day from being regarded as 'healthy' to 'Severe' in a moment. This was due to my 11-year-old daughter dying suddenly and unexpectedly, which caused my mental health to reach an all-time low. Before she died, my mental health was in the best shape it had ever been. I was a practising Buddhist and lived my life as mindfully as I could. I meditated twice daily, had a morning yoga ritual and attended meditation retreats. I was free from depression and anxiety and felt balanced and at peace. Then, following her sudden death, I experienced suicidal thoughts, hopelessness and helplessness. This exemplifies how a person's mental health can change quickly and drastically. Thankfully, it is a rare occurrence for a child to die, but it illustrates that it is impossible to predict what might have an impact on one's mental health. My daughter died at the school where I had been a teacher for 16 years, and therefore the trauma of this incident meant that I was unable to return to work there. Of course, there is no way to prepare mentally and physically for the disastrous effect an event like this has on a person's wellbeing. My daughter died five years ago now and I still have very desperately low moments, but I'm able to function in enough capacity to look after my family, form meaningful relationships and work as a lecturer. The main reason that I'm able to cope is because I know my limitations and have developed a mental self-awareness. I make sure that if I detect my mental health decreasing, I arm myself with certain strategies to ensure that I receive a necessary rise in wellbeing levels. For example, I spend time with one of my two surviving daughters and remind myself of the blessings I still have in my life. This is challenging at times due to my traditional 'glass half-empty' mindset, but I have discovered that learning to have a 'glass half-full' attitude is the only way I can survive. Other personal lifelines for me are distracting myself with work, helping others with mental health difficulties, especially related to bereavement, and pouring myself into writing this book, which has proven to be a therapy. If I am at home and find myself ruminating, then I've found that pulling out weeds from the garden seems to offer a temporary relief by easing some emotional pain. In addition, walking my dog at night along the dark streets flooded by streetlights gives

> *me a chance to cry in private and release some of the pent-up feelings and unhelpful emotions I feel, such as guilt and self-pity.*
>
> *Regardless of where you currently are, whether you are experiencing low levels of wellbeing or not, I urge you to develop the knowledge of what nurtures you and allows you to feel a sense of wellbeing and contentment so that you can help yourself in any moments of crisis. My purpose in sharing my sad story with you while discussing the mental health continuum is to urge you to never take your mental health for granted. Working on your own wellbeing is always an essential and worthwhile pursuit.*

What is stress and the signs of a dysfunctional workplace?

Stress is not technically a medical condition. Too much stress, or 'hyper-stress', causes 'distress', which will very negatively impact a teachers' wellbeing. Similarly, not enough stress, or 'hypo-stress', won't be ideal either, as this is caused by boredom or a lack of motivation. Therefore, it is useful for you to work towards having an optimum level of stress in your life, referred to as 'eustress' (which I think sounds like the name of a Disney Princess, but was coined by the Canadian physician Selye in 1976).

Most of us can cope with short bursts of stress, but research shows that prolonged bad stress is linked to mental health conditions such as anxiety and depression. The relationship between stress and mental health will be explored later in this chapter, along with an explanation of what stress does to our body and brain, including links to neuroscience. This section, however, is a brief explanation of how you can recognise stress in yourself and others so you can take the necessary action.

The Health and Safety Executive (HSE) define work-related stress as:

> the adverse reaction people have to excessive pressures or other types of demand placed on them at work.

If you are a school leader and you wish to watch over the workplace stress of your employees, I discuss the Workplace 'Management Standards' in Chapter 5. They will help you to recognise the reasons that underlie most stress in the workplace. Work Stress Network (n.d:7) lists the signs of a dysfunctional workplace and factors that could induce stress. If you wish to focus more on the positive, then as you read the list below, perhaps you could consider the opposite of each of the statements.

- use of technology to control, monitor and track workers
- the threat of or actual violence (verbal and/or physical abuse)
- lack of a clear job description or chain of command
- job insecurity
- lack of an understanding leadership
- cuts in national and local government funding leading to increased workloads
- long-hours culture
- no recognition or reward for good job performance
- no opportunity to voice complaints
- managers do not listen to and act upon concerns raised
- lack of employee representation and consultation
- lack of control or sufficient agency
- no opportunity to use personal talents or abilities
- inadequate time to complete tasks to personal or company standards
- unreasonable workload
- unremitting or prolonged pressures
- confusion caused by conflicting demands
- misuse of procedures (discipline/performance/absence)

We all cope with pressure in individual ways. This tends to be determined by a variety of factors, including our support systems at home and work, our personalities and whether we have any coping mechanisms in place to mitigate and alleviate our stress. It is important to realise and acknowledge that what may be too much pressure for one teacher at one particular time may not be too much for the same teacher at a different time or for a different teacher at any time (if that makes sense!?).

It is easy to know what stress does to us, but it is harder to recognise it in others as stress manifests in different ways. Keep guard for times when your colleagues are showing signs of stress, not so you can be a big know-it-all and say, 'you're stressed, you are!' but so you can keep a gentle eye on them. Peer support lessens isolation and provides a forum to discuss problems, such as disruptive pupils. Those are the times when you will need to stop, take stock and put some strategies in place. You will find suggested strategies in Part 2 of this book. I hope the checklist below, along with Figure 2.1 above, will enable you to distinguish and identify the signs of your, or a colleague's, wellbeing slipping below par:

Physical signs might include the following:

- Frequent absence from work.
- Being run-down and experiencing frequent minor illnesses.
- General aches and pains.
- Headaches.
- Difficulty sleeping or sleeping too much.
- Weight loss or gain (food cravings).
- Lack of care over appearance.
- Gastrointestinal disorders.
- Rashes/eczema.

Other signs might include the following:

- Difficulty remembering things and poor concentration (Now, where was I? ☺).
- Loss of confidence.
- Finding it difficult to make decisions.
- Overreacting to things.
- Unplanned absences.
- Arguments/conflicts with others—irritability, crying, shouting etc.
- Being quick to use grievance procedures.
- Loss of sense of humour.
- Increased errors and/or accidents.
- Taking on too much work and volunteering for every new project.
- Being adamant that they are right.
- Working too many hours—first in, last out/emailing out-of-hours or while on holiday.
- Being louder or more exuberant than usual.
- Overreliance on substances—alcohol, nicotine etc.
- Strained personal relationships.
- Withdrawn manner.
- Anxiety and depression (explored later in this chapter).
- Feeling burnt-out, constantly tired or exhausted.

What is burnout?

The World Health Organization (WHO) defines burnout as an occupational phenomenon and:

> a syndrome which is conceptualised as resulting from chronic workplace stress that has not been successfully managed.

Another definition of burnout is:

> a cognitive-emotional reaction to stress characterised by high levels of exhaustion resulting from the chronic demands made on a person's resources
>
> (Raedeke & Smith, 2009).

Burnout can be a gradual process so may be hard to recognise as the associated behaviour and feelings become habitual and unconscious. It affects different people in different ways but tends to present as someone feeling physically and emotionally 'off' after experiencing incessant stress and overwhelm. It generally has three elements:

- Energy depletion or exhaustion
- Increased mental distance from one's job or feelings of negativism or cynicism
- Reduced professional efficacy

Burnout can often happen when an intense workload meets other personal demands or non-work stresses. School leaders may not be aware of a staff's personal issues and so this can easily go undetected. The end point of burnout can often be numbness or a feeling of being frozen or detached from life. This manifests as someone not being able to move as their body literally takes over and pleads 'I can't take this anymore'. It is crucial to recognise that you are on the road to burnout before you get to this stage, which is something that I personally neglected to do. Therefore, along with the signs that demonstrate stress that I have mentioned above, it may be useful to ask yourself the following questions to find out if you are experiencing burnout:

- Am I connected to work that's important to me? (If you aren't, this may over time lead to burnout.)
- Am I refreshed after sleep and excited about the day ahead? (Constant tiredness or depressed feelings related to work could indicate burnout. Sleep changes are a strong initial indicator of ill health.)
- Am I unable to switch off from work-related matters, or am I mentally churning over work issues? (Not ever being able to leave work at work could be a sign of burnout.)
- How are the quality of my relationships? Am I isolating myself or constantly being irritated by people around me? (If your relationships are breaking down, then this could be due to the intense pressure you are feeling at work).
- Have I got Sunday night blues that go on for more than a couple of Sundays? (Obviously, everyone may feel this to a certain extent, but if you feel like this every Sunday for a long period, this may be an indicator of burnout).

Things to do if you think you have burnout:

- Get plenty of rest and spend extended time switching off from work completely. Try to keep in touch with work though, as it may not be helpful to isolate yourself at home.
- Seek professional help and/or contact your GP for advice.
- Identify the sources of your stress and take a good look at everything that's expected of you each day. Ask yourself if you can eliminate or adjust anything causing you undue pressure (often with the help of school leaders) so that you can stay in school but with a different role or responsibility. This may be only for a short amount of time until you regain your health.

Sadly, the hardest thing for many teachers is to disclose that they are experiencing difficulties without feeling a sense of failure, but there is no shame in admitting you could do with some help or some time away from work. Remember, we can't look after others until we look after ourselves, so we are being selfless to recognise that we need to seek support. If you are not resting over the weekend and not getting a chance to refresh, repair and rejuvenate, then stress will quite naturally occur, as we are only human. That's why we need to get a balance of work and rest, hence the next section about finding, achieving and sustaining a work-life balance.

What is work-life balance?

The solution to many things in life is balance. Incorporating balance into your life can nurture greater life fulfilment and can be achieved by focusing upon both pleasure and purpose. However, Buckingham & Goodall (2019) insist from their research that the happiest people are those striving for imbalance because they realise that balance is unachievable and causes unnecessary anxiety. They found that it's important to do what you enjoy and what is meaningful, but to do it now 'amongst the chaos'.

It is fair to say that whatever your thoughts are related to the idea of balance or imbalance, a bit of what's good and bad for us creates a healthy equilibrium to our lives, and that is what I mean here by 'balance'. If you work too extensively, it is clear that you will only be able to sustain this ongoing pressure of burning the candle at both ends for so long before it catches up with you and you risk getting ill. Having hobbies and interests tends to improve your productivity and job satisfaction, which is worth recalling when you opt to continue working (or marking books) instead of doing something more pleasurable. 'Me-time' helps us to keep life and our problems in perspective too. Don't work until you have no energy left to devote to pastimes or else you will just find yourself working and sleeping and nothing else in between.

A piece of feedback I received after a Teacher Wellbeing workshop I delivered demonstrated how easy it is to let work take over…

You've reminded me that I used to paint when things were getting too much—time to get in the loft and dig out my paints. Thank you!

We don't need more time; we need more space—mental and physical space—and the chance to breathe and experience freedom. Try to carve out a portion of your day dedicated to space. Ensure that you have the ideal balance to fit your life and that you are working to live, rather than living to work. I discuss strategies that you can adopt to work towards more balance in your personal and professional life in Chapter 3.

The science behind the stress response

I have found that by addressing the key information around wellbeing in a scientific way often gives it more credibility and legitimacy. Understanding the science behind our body's stress response can normalise our feelings and remind us that it's a natural reaction that everyone can relate to, thus decreasing our fear when it happens to us. That being said, when someone experiences symptoms of intense stress and overwhelm, especially for the first time, it can be extremely daunting and scary.

My wish is not to present stress as something to fear. I don't want to panic readers into fretting about what effect their long-term stress has had on their health. This cycle of becoming stressed about our stress is futile. Instead, I would like you to reflect upon the following idea:

When you change your mind about stress, and learn to fear it less, you can change your body's response to it (McGonigal, 2013).

An interesting idea, eh? And one that inspires optimism.

> *I have approached many therapists over the years for guidance on how to deal with my teacher stress, particularly my anxiety. Two pieces of advice stood out to me that related to whether one should fear stress or not. The first was after a session of reflexology, where I was floating in a relaxed state only to be given this warning by the therapist... she said that our bodies could be compared to an onion and each time we got stressed, a layer of onion was peeled off. If we experienced prolonged stress, she continued to explain, then we would expose the center of the onion and that was when illness would occur. All of my calm, joyous feelings from the reflexology disappeared as I ruminated on the damage I had probably done to my health by having experienced lengthy spells of stress at school. These thoughts, in response to this well-meaning advice, caused me extra stress and worry—especially when I saw an onion!*
>
> *The second and opposing piece of advice was from a therapist after a back, neck and shoulder massage. Again, I was floating in a state of relaxation even though, as I talked to her and glanced in the mirror, I was embarrassingly aware that a big oval mark had been indented onto my face by the face-hole on her massage table. Anyway, her advice was to embrace my anxiety as if it were an old friend and to thank it for giving me signs so*

> *I could amend my behaviour or thinking; she told me to interpret the letter 'x' in the spelling of anxiety as a kiss so I wouldn't forget this. I have found this to be useful advice during many times of stress at school. It has reinforced the idea that 'what we resist, persists (C.G. Jung). As such, I have slowly but surely learned to begin to accept my feelings of stress and hold them close as valuable indicators of when I need to stop or change my negative thoughts.*

McGonigal (2013) encourages us to look on our stress as helpful for our performance and as an energiser. McGonigal claims that chances are you will live longer if you learn to respond to your anxiety more favourably—sounds like good payback to me. In many ways, the stress response should be portrayed positively, as it is designed to protect us from danger so that we can react quicker in order to escape or fight. This is a supportive way to view our stress and may be helpful for you once you have gained an insight into what is happening in your body and why.

Feelings of stress in our body are designed to save our life (so that our ancient ancestors knew whether to fight, flight or freeze if a tiger was chasing them). Let's consider the basic science behind the stress response and how it can be defined. The stress response refers to a physiological reaction triggered by a real, imaginary or perceived threat; it occurs when something is terrifying to a person, either mentally or physically. This response is very rapid and happens unconsciously (Figure 2.2).

This body functioning was designed for short-term effect, or acute stress, so that you could escape quickly. However, if your body is under undue stress for long periods, ill health can result, either in the physical or emotional sense. Long-term stress can trap you in a negative cycle, but there is always a way out! In Part 2, I suggest some strategies to use to avoid this damaging cycle and ways to encourage the parasympathetic nervous system to take over. When you apply your 'check-in' (See Step 1) during teaching days, with practise and perseverance you will learn to recognise the initial signs usual to your body when it is responding to stress, for example tense muscles, dry mouth etc. The good news is, with a repetition of this self-regulation practice, you will then be able to choose which system your body uses. Using a proactive approach and early intervention, this 'check-in' will become your own best friend so you can stop the stress response in

- In response to acute stress, the amygdala (an area of the brain that controls our decision-making and emotional responses) sends an emergency signal to the hypothalamus. The hypothalamus is then stimulated, which is the command center of the brain which communicates with the rest of the body.

- This subsequently activates the sympathetic nervous system, suddenly releasing two hormones: adrenaline and non-adrenaline. These chemicals are made by our pituitary gland and the adrenal glands transport them all around your body when you are stressed.

- The adrenal cortex releases another chemical called cortisol, which helps you to stay alert and enables your body to maintain a steady supply of glucose. Have you heard of adrenal overload or fatigue which can result if someone has been dealing with excessive amounts of stress? That is because the immune system is suppressed when cortisol is being released.

- This then results in an increase in your heart rate, blood pressure and breathing rate, all in an attempt to get more energy and oxygen to your body. Your pupils even dilate to allow more light into the eyes, resulting in better vision of your surroundings, and your liver releases glucose to provide your body with energy. The sweat that appears on your palms is designed to improve our grip, so that we could climb a tree easily if we need to escape! The body is an amazing thing which deserves our respect; we realise that even more when we learn to appreciate how hard it works to try to keep us safe.

- The presence of cortisol reduces the immune system, and your digestive and reproductive system shuts down so that only the most basic body systems work so that you are able to run away quickly from whatever danger is imminent. The urge for sex is probably not in the forefront of your mind if a tiger was chasing you; therefore your reproductive system can take a back seat.

- It is worth valuing how this response can actually help you to perform better in situations when you need it, for example, adrenaline pumping through your body can give you that extra boost during a lesson observation but then may leave you feeling exhausted afterwards.

- After the threat has subsided, it takes the body up to an hour to return to its pre-arousal levels. The good news is that as we calm down from the threat of danger, our para sympathetic nervous system takes control and brings the body back into a balanced state. Switching to another nervous system is your body's way to come down from the stress and let you know that the danger has passed and there's nothing to be afraid of anymore.

- Your digestive system starts working well to signal you to eat again. Your reproductive system works effectively again to signal you to... well, to do that, if the mood takes you, now a tiger is no longer chasing you!

- Your heart rate slows down, blood moves away from the muscles and you relax. However, if fear continues then this signals to the amygdala and the process starts all over again.

Figure 2.2 The stress response.

its tracks, meaning that it rarely develops into a full-blown stress attack. It is annoying though, because as humans, our default mode is for the sympathetic nervous system to become stimulated rather than the wonderful parasympathetic nervous system. In other words, our inherent disposition is to think negatively and to worry and fret. But more about this in the below section, 'Is happiness in the mind?' In the stress-response process I have described above, serotonin (a feel-good chemical) is reduced, which, if left untreated, can lead to poor mental health. Stress is not always a precursor for you to have poor mental health, though.

Anxiety and depression are the most common mental health problems in the UK. Now that you are reading this book, though, and are keen to address your wellbeing, you will be prepared for this eventuality and geared up to recognise anxiety as your internal warning system. One in four people in the UK have been found to have a diagnosable mental health problem at some point, and a further 18% said they'd suffered with a non-diagnosed mental health illness (Health Survey for England, 2014). However, most difficulties tend to be short-term and are often successfully treated. I like to use the simile that anxiety is like the passing rain clouds in the sky and depression is like the sky when it is thick with clouds. However, with both conditions it is important to remember that there is the chance of a blue, clear sky just around the corner; although, it's important to acknowledge that recovery can be difficult to fathom when you are in the midst of either an anxiety attack or severe depression.

What is anxiety?

Anxiety is the most common mental health condition. It is a normal, natural response to fear; we experience it when faced with situations we find threatening or difficult. Anxiety can be described as feeling worried, uneasy or fearful. Some people find it hard to control their worries; their feelings of anxiety are more constant and often affect their daily lives. Anxiety can have both psychological and physical symptoms. Anxiety is labelled as an anxiety disorder, such as social phobia or obsessive-compulsive disorder, if the presence of it affects your day-to-day functioning and stops you from living the life you wish to.

Psychologists believe that anxiety is maintained by a vicious circle of thoughts, beliefs, behaviours and feelings. The treatment of Cognitive

Behavioural Therapy (CBT) is based upon challenging this type of thinking. For example, consider this scenario, that I've named the 'Supermarket Scenario':

Let's imagine that I met you at a party and we connected and enjoyed each other's company. Then, the next day, you saw me across a supermarket carpark. You waved, and I ignored you. Chances are, you would feel confused and have negative thoughts about me, despite the night before. This experience may induce anxiety and insecurity in you, especially if you saw me again and I reacted the same way, which might trigger negative behaviour in you (maybe a rude gesture!?). It may remind you of a time in your life previously when someone had shunned you or you had felt ignored. However, if you reflected upon this incident from a positive standpoint you would see that there are numerous explanations for why I ignored you; for example, I may not have recognised you, I am short-sighted and therefore didn't see you or I was too distracted to notice you. In your anxious state and from a place of low confidence, you had assumed that I didn't like you. Anxiety often stops logical thinking in its tracks and causes irrational thinking patterns. Anxiety can result from the impact of previous anxious experiences that otherwise would have been harmless situations. The 'what ifs' that dominate an anxious mind can take over and sabotage, demonstrating that anxiety can often be more about perception than reality.

Examples of anxiety symptoms in the mind are:

- Feeling worried all the time,
- Being unable to concentrate,
- Feeling irritable etc.

Examples of anxiety symptoms in the body are:

- Irregular heartbeats (palpitations),
- Sweating,
- Muscle tension and pains,
- Breathing heavily,
- Dizziness,
- Indigestion or nausea.

These symptoms are easily mistaken by anxious people as evidence of serious physical illness, and their worry about this can make the symptoms even worse. Sudden unexpected surges of anxiety are called panic and usually lead to the person having to quickly get out of whatever situation they happen to be in. Anxiety and panic are often accompanied by feelings of depression, when we feel deeply sad, lose our appetite and see the future as bleak and hopeless. In fact, research has found that the same neurotransmitters are involved in both anxiety and depression; so, a person can be presenting with anxious depression (where depression is most dominant) or depressed anxiety.

A panic attack is simply an exaggeration of the body's normal 'fight or flight' reaction. It can be very alarming for the sufferer and can last from five to twenty minutes. Often a panic attack can be mistaken for a heart attack as it shares many common symptoms, such as shortness of breath, chest pains and tingling. I have heard of incidents where teachers have experienced panic attacks so severe that an ambulance has had to be called to the school.

Step 4: Analysing fear and panic

This step is for a teacher who commonly experiences anxiety and/or depression at work. Writing down your feelings related to anxiety or depression may help you to understand what is contributing either to your fear and panic, or your sadness.

What is depression?

Depression can be mild and short-lived, or it can be severe and long-lasting. Depression is a pervasive and persistent feeling of sadness. Often the sufferer loses interest and joy in things they used to enjoy and find fulfilling. Depression interferes with daily life and often affects relationships and one's ability to work.

The charity Sane describes it as:

> a heavy weight, an emptiness, despair, hopelessness, as if the life source or spirit has been extinguished.

Depression can cause a wide range of symptoms and affects people in a variety of ways. Many people feel tearful and experience physical affects too, such as tiredness, having no appetite and aches and pains.

Examples of depressive symptoms in the body:

- Feeling tired and lacking energy
- Low or no libido
- Experiencing changes in sleeping patterns (too much/not enough)
- Experiencing changes in appetite (greater or less than normal)

Examples of depressive symptoms in the mind:

- Feeling in a low mood for long periods of time
- Feeling restless, agitated or irritable
- Feeling guilty and worthless
- Feeling numb and empty
- Feeling hopeless and helpless
- Getting no pleasure from previously enjoyable activities
- Losing self-confidence and self-esteem
- Wanting to withdraw from people
- Finding it hard to concentrate
- Being preoccupied by negative thoughts
- Thoughts about self-harm
- Having suicidal thoughts

Gaining control of your mind and attempting to understand and reverse negative thought patterns may help you as a teacher.

Is happiness in the mind?

Thich Nhat Hanh (2017: xxvi) writes that 'happiness is a habit that each of us needs to learn.' He believes that it is possible to cultivate happiness by training the mind. Many people advocate mindfulness as a tool to gain more control over the mind. Mindfulness could be portrayed as a buzzword, something that is bandied around as a quick fix to happiness and living in the present moment. However, it is far from a quick fix. It is exceptionally difficult to let go of past thoughts and future ruminations and settle into the present, but it is possible. It is a lifelong process and takes patience and perseverance, but the rewards are great and many. A section in Chapter

4 guides you through the basics of mindfulness. Once you've read about it, you can decide whether it is a practice that suits you or not.

Our perceptions and the way our mind processes our experiences can affect how stressful a situation is to us, how stressful it continues to be and how much it interferes with our health and wellbeing. The power appears to therefore lie within our mind and our ability to control our responses to certain situations, like how we react to the Supermarket Scenario mentioned previously. Nevertheless, I can hear you screaming that you have many external factors that cause and contribute to your stress and that these are outside of your control or mind. This may be true, but the way that you react to stress has a massive bearing on your wellbeing, and that's the bit you do have control over! We all know how negative self-talk can compound our suffering and has a 'powerful impact on emotional wellbeing and motivation' (Braiker, 1989:23). Therefore, we need to stop negative internal chatter from becoming an unconscious habit and only listen and respond to the accurate self-talk that doesn't overgeneralise and exaggerate the negatives.

> *I remember once when a very special Buddhist monk I know advised me to record my mental self-talk during three hours of my day. He instructed me to place a grey pebble in my pocket for every negative thought I had about myself, and a white pebble in my pocket for every positive affirmation. I was then able to see how many grey pebbles superseded the white ones, which was what I had expected. In fact, to my dismay, there were over four times as many grey pebbles, as white (I had 62 black and 14 white pebbles). Perhaps you could try this?*
>
> *Having established how much I berate myself with self-defeating and erroneous self-talk (four times as much as I notice good things about myself) I decided to try to notice this consciously and attempt to regularly challenge it as much as I could. As it happened, I got the perfect opportunity to do this very soon after, when something embarrassing happened during one of my Monday afternoon teaching sessions…*
>
> *I was teaching the topic World War II to a class of Year 4 pupils. I am a fan of 'real audience' lessons where you create a situation for children to problem-solve as if they are actually experiencing it as a real-life challenge. The learning objective for that day was for the children to understand what a WWII blackout was. The lesson involved me firstly emitting an air raid siren noise and then explaining to the class that we needed to*

blackout the classroom windows quickly to make sure we were safe. Everything worked as expected; excitedly the class began using teamwork skills to cover the windows with black paper, but in their frenzy and haste, one of the girls accidently hit the fire alarm button in the corner of the room with her elbow (unbeknownst to me at the time). The fire alarm sounded and of course the whole school (at least 650 children and 40 school staff!) began exiting the school buildings, congregating on the field. I noticed a disgruntled look on the Headteacher's face as he passed my classroom window—I saw it from a crack in the only window that hadn't been blacked-out by paper. My class started filing out of the classroom and, as I reached the field, I heard whispers of 'Who's set the alarm off?' Unfortunately, one of the reception classes had been changing for P.E. when the alarm began and so many small children were in different states of dress and undress (and it was a cold February day!).

The Headteacher was pacing up and down, looking angry while he questioned the confused site manager who then returned into school to check which classroom had triggered the alarm. By this time, the constant whisper of 'Sonia set off the alarm' reached me from my class's line and so I had a few anxious moments of waiting for the site manager to appear. When he did, it was obvious that I was to blame as he looked over in my direction giving me a displeased stare. The Headteacher then shouted, 'false alarm everyone, please return to your classrooms!' and began striding towards me. He reprimanded me in front of my class, which was quite humiliating, by shouting:

> Mrs Allies, someone in your class set off the alarm. Can you find out who this was and explain to them the inconvenience that this has caused? Please keep better control of your class in the future.

I recall that I started mumbling something about how the lesson had been about the blackout and how engaged the children had been. This didn't make a difference to his demeanour. He headed back to his office, tutting and shaking his head, leaving my class laughing at the way I had been 'told-off' by the Headteacher! The only child that wasn't laughing at me was Sonia.

So, I admit, my negative self-talk after this incident went like this:

'You are a dreadful teacher and hopeless at controlling children. The Headteacher obviously thinks you are rubbish now and irresponsible. He will hate you forever etc.' (which equalled five grey pebbles!)

I am proud to say by this stage in my teaching career, I was beginning to perfect the art of mindfulness, so I challenged these thoughts with:

> 'You were only trying to plan an exciting lesson. It wasn't your fault that Sonia hit the alarm button. This isn't a reflection of your teaching. Don't blame yourself. Next time I teach this lesson, I will remind the pupils to be careful of the fire alarm button', (which equalled five white pebbles, to counteract the grey ones!).

Step 5: Stop and drop negative thoughts

A simple technique that has worked for me when I try to challenge my negative self-talk is the following:

When something goes wrong, rather than using language such as, 'I should have...', 'I always...' or 'I wish I'd...', I would use, 'Next time I will...', as this accentuated the learning that I had taken from the situation, which feels more positive and empowering than merely turning the situation against myself. It stops the negative downward spiral in its tracks and gives a viable option for the future.

When we worry or ruminate over situations that we wish had been different, then we are living in the past; when we worry about what's to come, then we are living in the future. Eckhart Tolle (2016) in his inspirational book 'The Power of Now' reminds us that the most precious moment is the only one that's important and that's the present moment. Focusing our attention on our present moment will allow us to relax and find peace.

> When I went to my GP about 15 years ago with depression and anxiety, he mentioned meditation as a possible strategy and my first thought was, 'No! How can that help? I want medication, not meditation!' However, I can't emphasise enough how helpful meditation and mindfulness practices have been for me over the years. I have found it very useful in quieting the internal chatter in my mind. It allows me to stop momentarily and escape from negative self-talk and worry...
>
> There were many days when I got to lunchtime feeling as if I had been pulled through a hedge backwards. The nonstop mornings that I often had as a primary school teacher would leave me in what I referred to as a 'jingly jangly' state come lunchtime. For example, a morning usually consisted of the following:
>
> - getting my three children up and ready for school,
> - getting my classroom organised for the day,

- grabbing the TA to go over the morning's work,
- settling nearly 200 children on the playground under the watchful eyes of masses of parents,
- teaching the first lesson,
- doing playground duty,
- teaching the second lesson and worrying about the marking that had just mounted up from those two lessons.

It was lunchtime before I realised that I hadn't stopped at all since 6:00am. So, at 12:30pm, in order to reset, I would disappear into the toilet cubical and sit on the toilet (with the seat down!), close my eyes and breathe. I would focus on deep breathing for about one minute, and then I would do a quick body-scan for about two minutes. Then, I would spend about three minutes breathing out my negative cluttered thoughts by imagining them leaving my body and mind as dark smoke with every out-breath. I would then visualise that with every in-breath, I was breathing in a positive, relaxing and calming white light. I emerged about nine minutes later feeling like a different person. I felt rejuvenated and refreshed, ready to start the afternoon despite encountering the long queue of staff waiting outside for the toilet cubical that I had occupied for those nine minutes!

Don't get me wrong, for those nine minutes it was difficult to turn off thoughts like, 'you haven't got the resources ready for your next lesson', 'why are you wasting nine minutes doing nothing?', but I soon realised that those nine minutes were the most important of my day. They helped me relieve myself from the stress that had accumulated from the morning. In addition, those nine minutes made me a more patient and responsive (rather than reactive) teacher than I otherwise would have been for the rest of the day. It may have even made me a better parent in the evening.

When my oldest daughter was seven, she presented me with a decorated plaque for my bedroom door that stated, 'Please don't disturb me, I'm meditating.' She explained that I could stick it on my door so everyone in my family would keep out. I found out that this gift wasn't purely altruistic when she further elaborated: 'You're a much nicer mummy after you've been meditating'—out of the mouths of babes!

The reason why present-moment awareness is so difficult to master is because the brain works in ways that make our bad habits very difficult to eliminate or reverse. You see, our reptilian brains are geared up for self-sabotage; neuroscientists describe this as a negativity bias or the default mode of our brain, as I've already mentioned. Each habit presents as a succession of thoughts that cluster together to form a neural pathway. The more thoughts you add to this habit, the thicker it gets and the harder it is to build a new habit that is stronger than the last one. Some teachers can have a propensity to overestimate the threats in their daily lives and underestimate the rewards. As Burch & Penman (2013:158) state, many teachers struggle with negative thinking and can:

> tend to see threats everywhere and notice the flaws in everything… we simply do not notice the overwhelming number of pleasant things in our lives.

A clever neuroscientist, Dr Hanson (2009), describes this as the brain possessing 'Velcro for negative experiences and Teflon for good ones.'

However, the good news from neuroscience is this idea of 'neuroplasticity', which means that the brain is malleable and can create new neural connections, and therefore we are able to develop new habits of thinking. These new habits should trigger the comfort system rather than the threat system thus allowing us to rewire our brains with lots of practice and reinforcement. It might be useful for you to think about how anxiety keeps us in our heads, but that we can move from head to heart with some positive affirmations and developing a conscious habit to direct some love towards ourselves. Sammons (2019) encourages us to ignite the sooth-system of our brain rather than the threat-system. He advises that we talk to ourselves with kindness and compassion as we would hope our best friend would do. This technique is called Compassion Focused Therapy (CFT), and Sammons cites this as the way that teachers can deal with their daily mental stress.

Sacks (2017) writes about how useful meditation and mindfulness are for our brains. He discusses that the comfort system in our brain is triggered when we meditate and so, even if we are finding it hard to meditate, knowing it is there for you is a comforting thought. There is a strong evidence-base supporting the scientific health benefits of meditation. For instance, a few minutes of conscious deep-belly breathing can massage our vagus nerve, which enables the parasympathetic nervous system to release anti-stress enzymes and calming hormones, such as oxytocin. There is more about the practical application of mindfulness in Chapter 4.

How's my wellbeing?

I am utilising the findings of a Gallup poll that comprehensively studied people in more than 150 countries and revealed five universal, interconnected elements that shape our lives: Physical Wellbeing, Career Wellbeing, Social Wellbeing and Community Wellbeing. I have added Emotional Wellbeing as a category and omitted Financial Wellbeing, as that is a specialist field and outside of my remit. If you feel that you need help to manage your economic life in order to reduce stress and feel financially secure, then refer to help online or from your Local Citizen's Advice Bureau.

The 'How's my wellbeing?' assessment below is intended for you to begin to informally gauge your levels of wellbeing. It contains questions to get you thinking so you can initially pinpoint a wellbeing area to concentrate on or rank the areas according to those you feel more positively towards. The questions are based on general recommendations from a variety of sources related to each wellbeing area. Please don't take too much heed to the questions, as I have found that wellbeing recommendations change constantly, for example, the amount of fruit and vegetables we should eat daily changes from one day to the next, just as coffee can be considered good for you one minute and bad for you the next. So, like I mentioned, *you* are best placed to decide what seems to impact your wellbeing positively or negatively, as you are basing this information on the experiences of living with yourself for as long as you have!

By calculating a score for your wellbeing, you can ascertain if your wellbeing is currently at a low, medium or high level. It should also highlight to you if there is a certain area of your life you should devote more attention to, for example, your physical wellbeing (Table 2.1).

Useful resources

- The website www.workstress.net offers information about laws and regulations related to stress at work.

Takeaway message: Which school strategies support teacher wellbeing?

As we move towards thinking about practical strategies for wellbeing, it is worth guessing what the four school-based strategies that Glazzard's (2019)

Table 2.1 How's my wellbeing? A general assessment (Visit my website: www.supportingteacherwellbeing.wordpress.com to download this assessment).

	Main question:	Scores (out of...)	Questions to ask yourself to inform your answer/further information/notes:
General wellbeing	How would you assess your current mental health? (If 10 is excellent and 0 is very poor)	10	
	How would you assess your current physical health? (If 10 is excellent and 0 is very poor)	10	
Area of wellbeing			
PHYSICAL— Having good health and enough energy to achieve what you want to. Sleep, food/ water and exercise	How much **sleep** do you get (on average) per night? If you get more than 7 hours, score 3 If you get between 6 and 7 hours, score 2 If you get between 5 and 6 hours, score 1 If you get under 5 hours, score 0	3	Generally, the recommended amount of sleep we should aim to get each night is at least 7 hours. Evidence demonstrates that the brain needs sleep to remain healthy. To assess whether you are getting enough sleep, ask yourself: How refreshed do I feel in the morning? Do I feel alert and ready to face the day, or groggy and irritable?
	How many **fruits or vegetables** are you eating each day? If you eat more than 5 fruits and vegetables, score 3 If you eat between 3-5 fruits and vegetables, score 2 If you eat 1-3 fruits and vegetables, score 1 If you eat no fruits or vegetables, score 0	3	Does my diet include a balance of protein, carbohydrates and healthy fats? Do my meals look colourful on the plate, or do I eat a lot of beige-coloured food? Do I eat a variety of fruits and vegetables? Do I eat each type of fruit and vegetable when it is in season, so I am consuming them at the freshest times and therefore getting the most nutrients?
	How much **water** do you drink a day? If you drink at least 1.5 litres of water a day (about 6 large glasses), score 3 If you drink between 4-6 large glasses of water a day, score 2 If you drink between 3-4 large glasses of water per day, score 1 If you drink under 3 large glass of water per day, score 0	3	Staying hydrated is useful for our physical health, mood and mental wellbeing. The amount you should drink is dependent on your current climate, activity levels, age, weight and health. Our food is thought to contribute about 20% of our fluid intake. Drinking at times when we start to feel thirsty is important; don't force yourself to drink if you don't feel thirsty. It is not clear exactly how much water we need; general advice states that the average person needs about 1.5 litres a day. It is best not to drink at the same time as eating, as your body absorbs the nutrients from the food more efficiently without food and allows water to penetrate cells more easily.
	What **exercise** do you engage in each week? If you exercise exactly as the NHS specifies, score 3 If you exercise mostly as the NHS specifies, score 2 If you exercise sometimes as the NHS specifies, score 1 If you never exercise as the NHS specifies, score 0	3	The NHS recommends the following: • aim to be physically active every day and reduce the time spent sitting or lying down with activity. • do strengthening activities that work all the major muscles at least 2 days a week • do at least 150 minutes of moderate-intensity activity a week or 75 minutes of vigorous intensity activity a week It specifies that: 'you can do your weekly target of physical activity on a single day or over 2 or more days. Whatever suits you.'

(Continued)

Table 2.1 Continued

	Main question:	Scores (out of...)	Questions to ask yourself to inform your answer/further information/notes:
EMOTIONAL—Ability to manage your emotions successfully and deal with change	How easily do you manage your emotions? 'Very easily', score 3 'Easily', score 2 'It depends', score 1 'Not at all', score 0	3	What do I do when I feel low? Do I find it easy or difficult to show my feelings? Can I communicate my feelings to others? Who do I share my feelings with? Have I anyone at work that I can talk to about my feelings? Do I enjoy solitude and spend adequate time alone?
	How successfully do you deal with change? 'Very well', score 3 'Well', s3core 2 'It depends', score 1 'Not at all', score 0	3	Do I feel excited, neutral or fearful when faced with change?
CAREER—Enjoying your job and finding meaning and satisfaction via it	Do you enjoy your job? 'I love it', score 3 'I like it', score 2 'It's ok, I suppose', score 1 'I hate it', score 0	3	Do I feel motivated by teaching or my work in school? Do I feel valued by management? Do I feel seen, heard and cared for at work? Am I excited to go to work most days? Do I feel overwhelmed by my workload? Do I feel able to manage the behaviour of my class?
	Do you find meaning and satisfaction in your job? 'Yes, definitely!', score 3 'Yes, I do', score 2 'A little bit', score 1 'No', score 0	3	Do I feel a sense of purpose in what I do? Do I feel comfortable in the work environment, e.g. is it clean and conducive to learning etc. Do I have a best friend at work? Can I list the reasons that made me choose a career in teaching? Does my job parallel my life values?
SOCIAL—Having supportive relationships and hobbies and interests	Have you got people in your life that support and nurture you and offer quality relationships? 'Yes, lots of them', score 3 'Yes, quite a lot', score 2 'Only a few', score 1 'No', score 0	3	Am I listened to by people that are close to me? Who do I turn to in times of need? What characteristics do I need most in a friend? Why? Do I feel valued and needed by those around me? Do I regularly spend quality time with friends and/or family?
	Have you got interests and hobbies that you engage you outside of work? 'Yes, I'm always doing something that I enjoy', score 3 'Yes, I have quite a lot of hobbies and interests', score 2 'I have a few that I enjoy', score 1 'No', score 0	3	Do I spend time engaging in hobbies and interests that fulfil me? Do I have downtime every evening?

WHAT DO YOU NEED TO KNOW ABOUT WELLBEING?

COMMUNITY — Liking your environment and where you live and feeling safe with a sense of belonging	Do you like the environment where you live? 'I love it', score 3 'I like it', score 2 'It's okay', score 1 'No', score 0	Am I proud of my surroundings and take pride in my house/flat etc.? Do I get a sense of accomplishment when I do the housework?	3
	Do you feel safe where you live and feel you belong? 'Yes, I feel very safe', score 3 'Yes, I feel safe', score 2 'I feel quite safe', score 1 'No', score 0	Do I feel relaxed where I live? Do I have a sense of community and belonging? Do I worry about the safety of myself or my possessions?	3
		Score out of 56	

Record your 'How's my wellbeing?' scores:
GENERAL WELLBEING (out of 20) =
PHYSICAL WELLBEING (out of 12) =
EMOTIONAL WELLBEING (out of 6) =
CAREER WELLBEING (out of 6) =
SOCIAL WELLBEING (out of 6) =
COMMUNITY WELLBEING (out of 6) =
Total: (out of 56) =
Is there an area that stands out for you as…
A strength?
An area for development?

If you scored between **0–20**, then you need to begin to have more of a strong focus on your wellbeing as a teacher. I recommend that you read all of my chapters thoroughly and try to incorporate as much of the guidance, advice, strategies and recommended resources as you can. After about a month's time, it would be useful to complete this assessment again to check that you are gaining better wellbeing. If not, it might be worth visiting your GP to seek professional help with your mental and physical health.

If you scored between **21–45**, then your wellbeing appears to be at a medium level. However, there are areas that you could improve upon to ensure that you are operating in a healthy way both for your body and mind. Maintaining a full focus on your wellbeing is the only way for you to thrive as a teacher and fulfil your full potential. It is crucial that you are having 'time out' to rest or to pursue your hobbies or interests. Try to ascertain which areas you scored the lowest on and focus on improving those areas by reading the related chapters most thoroughly and taking the 'Useful resources' into account.

If you scored between **46–56**, then your wellbeing is obviously something that you prioritise. You could still look at the areas where you scored the lowest and see if there is anything you can incorporate so that your wellbeing is even better. It is important not to take your mental health and wellbeing for granted, so keep a focus on how you support yourself as a teacher, and if your wellbeing does dip, then make sure you have contingency plans in place for communicating this and knowing where you would go for help.

participants felt best supported their teacher wellbeing. Have a think, and then look at the list below for the answers…

They were:

- a wellbeing policy for staff,
- buddying support from colleagues,
- an open culture related to wellbeing throughout the school (which is driven by the Headteacher),
- performance management targets focused on wellbeing.

Were you right? All of these initiatives are discussed further in Parts 2 and 3.

PART 2

STRATEGIES FOR WELLBEING

3

WHICH WORK-LIFE BALANCE STRATEGIES BEST SUPPORT WELLBEING?

Work-life balance in early-career teachers

This chapter will introduce you to a plethora of strategies related to wellbeing and work-life balance that can be applied to your job as a teacher. It utilises two very different case studies of early-career teachers; one from a teacher who successfully manages to maintain a work-life balance, and one from another teacher who fails miserably. Early-career teachers have been found to be particularly vulnerable to mental health problems. For example, the 'Teacher Wellbeing Index' (ESP, 2019:36) reported that Newly Qualified Teachers (NQTs) suffered the most mental health issues (43%) compared to teachers generally (35%). They also found that staff working for zero to five years experienced more symptoms related to panic attacks. To counteract this, the study proposed that personal mental health and wellbeing training should be statutory within Initial Teacher Training. This seems a worthy venture, especially as the study reported that 52% of NQTs and those in the profession under five years had recently considered leaving due to health issues and low wellbeing. Rogers (2018) writes,

To stop our NQTs from fleeing the classroom, we must offer words of encouragement, meet with them regularly and reassure them that they won't get everything right first time around.

Although, a variety of strategies will be shared in this chapter, it is worth remembering that the kind of wellbeing strategies that are effective do vary considerably from one person to another.

> For example, one of my friends really enjoys massages and saves up so that she can indulge in a deep tissue massage twice a month. I concur with this and regularly use my handheld massager to penetrate and loosen the tight muscles that build up in my trapezius, shoulders and neck. This has lessened my occurrence of headaches due to muscular tension. However, I have another friend who finds having a massage a traumatic and unenjoyable experience.
>
> Recently, I discovered how differently people feel about what qualifies as wellbeing to them when I used my Tibetan singing bowl in a wellbeing workshop for teachers. The singing bowl was designed to evoke feelings of calm and peace in the room and most of the delegates found this a pleasant sound and were eager to try to use it themselves. However, there was one teacher who found the experience akin to having someone scrape their fingernails down a blackboard! The realisation that, contrary to what I had assumed, not everybody in the room had appreciated the sound of my singing bowl made me appreciate how different we all are in many respects, but certainly in terms of what makes us feel good. I do recommend trying a wellbeing strategy at least once, though, so you can make an informed decision, as you never know exactly how something will affect you without direct, first-hand experience of it.

Case study 1: Getting it wrong—The story of Jen

As you read about Jen's life, reflect upon any similarities or differences to your life. Perhaps you may like to pretend you are Jen's life coach. What questions would you ask her and what advice would you offer?

Jen has been teaching for three years. She teaches a Year 1 class in an inner-city three-form entry school. She is single and lives in a flat with one female housemate (an international student training towards a degree in economics).

- Jen's alarm wakes her at 6.30 am. She hurriedly dresses. She doesn't have time to apply make-up and often wears the same black trousers and white shirt most days to work. She drives through traffic and doesn't have time for breakfast.
- Jen arrives at school at 7.30am and leaves all of her preparation for the day until then. If the photocopier is not working, she feels stressed. She usually spends half an hour talking to a teacher in the parallel class, but this usually involves a conversation about how stressed they are feeling.
- Jen works or marks through lunch and break. She has had three cups of coffee by lunchtime.
- She has a packed lunch for dinner which usually involves crisps, a can of pop, an apple and a yogurt that she grabs from the fridge. She eats in the classroom while she is preparing for the afternoon and constantly gets interrupted by pupils.
- She feels tired and stressed throughout the day and often shouts at her pupils; she suffers with sore throats. Children are confused by her lack of consistency with behaviour management.
- Her TA lacks direction in the classroom; Jen can just about keep up with what she is doing throughout the day, let alone directing another person.
- Parents find her hard to communicate with and defensive. Jen perceives parents as ungrateful and negative.
- Jen is a perfectionist and often sets herself unrealistic goals. This leads to a decrease in her self-confidence.
- Jen has been ill four times in the last six months. When she feels poorly, she pushes herself to come into work (she doesn't want to let anyone down).
- Jen leaves school at 6pm and takes at least two sets of children's books home. She marks books until 9pm.
- She is too tired in the evenings and weekends and so does not meet friends or socialise. She doesn't spend time with her housemate either. Sometimes she watches TV while drinking wine and eating chocolate. Jen often falls asleep on the sofa.
- Weekends are spent preparing lessons and doing her housework/shopping. Occasionally, she meets a friend (another stressed teacher) who saps her energy and keeps her feeling negative.
- Holidays are spent revising lesson plans and arranging her classroom ready for the next academic year. Jen hasn't been on a holiday in three years.

Case study 2: Getting it right—the story of Ollie

As you read about Ollie's life, reflect upon any similarities or differences to your life. Perhaps you may like to pretend you are interviewing Ollie for a local newspaper about how he balances his home and work life with a small child. What questions would you ask him about his life?

Ollie has been teaching for five years. He teaches a Year 5 class. He married last year and has a son who is six months old. His wife has recently started working two days a week and so their son is dropped off (by her) at the local childminders.

- Ollie arrives at school at 8am. He cycles to the station and catches the train to work. On the train, he browses lesson plans for the day on his iPad and prepares himself mentally. He writes a list of a few jobs for his TA, Tina, and then spends the rest of the journey eating a healthy breakfast (of porridge and blueberries), closing his eyes and relaxing and eating mindfully.
- Once at school, he makes sure he fills up his water bottle and gets time to catch up with Tina before the children arrive by looking at the plans for the day and arranging a time during the morning when they can both have 10 minutes of non-contact time.
- Ollie and Tina have a close relationship and share the same sense of humour. Tina is happy to give pupils verbal feedback in English lessons as she is confident in literacy. She assesses children throughout maths and science lessons and records any misconceptions she observes for Ollie. This kind of practice empowers Tina.
- Break-time is spent quickly setting up the next lesson with Tina (who knows what needs doing) and then Ollie has a rest, drink and chat in the staffroom.
- At lunchtime, he either has a mindful walk and some fresh air by walking to the local shop or pays £3 for a cooked school dinner.
- Ollie limits teacher-talk and ensures his lessons are as child-centred as possible. He utilises peer and self-assessment, which limits his marking. He frequently uses verbal feedback as a marking strategy and often spends the last 10 minutes of lessons giving immediate verbal feedback to pupils (with the help of Tina).
- The parents of his class respond well to his sense of humour and honest and caring approach.

- If Ollie feels ill, he lets his senior management team know as soon as possible to allow them to plan for cover. He has noticed that since his son has been going to the childminder, he has been more prone to catching colds. However, he has a sensible attitude towards this and rests, drinks plenty (of water!), eats lots of fruit and vegetables and listens to his body when he feels overwhelmed.
- His wife teaches yoga one night a week and so he attends her class (and luckily takes his son to his parent's house that evening). He has found it difficult to ask for help from his parents but knows that it is good for his son to have time away from his parents, and for him and his wife to have quality time alone.
- Ollie usually leaves school by 5.30pm at the latest. Before he leaves, he sets up class ready for the first lesson of the next day. He thoroughly marks only <u>one</u> set of books per night. He ensures that he plans a low-key lesson first thing on a Thursday as, due to staff meetings on a Wednesday night, he has less time to set up his classroom.
- On the train ride home, Ollie rests, relaxes and reacclimatises to his home-life. He phones his wife and makes plans for the evening, including what they are having for tea: They get their groceries delivered (£1 delivery slot) and compile a meal plan for the week.
- Saturday mornings are always spent planning for his week ahead. When planning, he realises that he needs a structure but one that can be adapted. As soon as it gets to 12.00pm on a Saturday, he stops work and spends time with friends or family. He attends a gym, goes running and cycling with friends or walks his dog on a Saturday afternoon/evening. Every other Sunday, Ollie has a lie-in (on a rota with his wife) and ensures that the remainder of Sunday is sacred time devoted entirely to his wife and son. Sometimes he checks his emails from 6pm until 7pm on a Sunday, as his wife takes their son to spend time with her sister and she prefers to visit alone.
- Ollie and his wife have a house rule that technology stays downstairs. Therefore, phones and iPads are charged in the kitchen and banned from the bedroom. They watch television together, especially a comedy series. Laughing seems to support their wellbeing, as does cuddling on the sofa while they are watching it.
- Every year, Ollie plans a holiday that he looks forward to and also spends time catching up with his family. He spends the first week of the

holiday getting the classroom ready for the next academic year and then forgets work for a month and enjoys spending time with his son and wife. Often, during the holidays, he visits his wife's family and they look after his son so that he has time to relax and unwind. He enjoys the creature comforts of staying with them because he gets a break from mundane tasks.

What key themes emerge for you when you read both case studies, for instance, how do each of them approach their personal time? Although it seems unfair to compare like with like, there are lessons to learn from each approach. Perhaps you reflected upon the following themes while you were reading the case studies:

- **Organisation**: Ollie ensures he is one step ahead with work and home-life routines. Jen is more unorganised with her time.
- **'Me' time**: Ollie ensures that he has down-time to relax and enjoy the aspects of life that nurture him, including regular exercise. Ollie socialises regularly, but Jen does not prioritise time for herself or allow for good company. Ollie makes sure that he has time during the year where he holidays and explores non-work activities.
- **Regular breaks**: Ollie ensures that he has slower-paced periods in his day whereas Jen maintains a fast-paced frantic schedule, leaving little time for rest.
- **Eating**: Ollie is well-prepared with nourishing snacks and ensures that he is hydrated. Jen relies on caffeine and convenience foods.
- **Perfectionism**: Jen demands unrealistic high expectations of herself that ultimately frustrate her and negatively affect her self-image. Ollie puts less pressure on himself and has a realistic attitude about what he can accomplish.

Work-life balance: Finding your way to achieve balance

Work-life balance emerged as the top issue at work for 69% of education professionals (ESP, 'Teacher Wellbeing Index', 2019). Many teachers admitted to finding the balance between home and work difficult to manage. This stress may be causing teachers to experience relationship issues; by having to complete paperwork out of school hours, this may be stopping them from spending time with their family.

In the 'Teacher Wellbeing Index' (ESP, 2019), teachers were asked to identify the factors that contributed to a negative work-life balance and they most commonly indicated that this was the inability to switch off and relax (74%). Having a work-life balance was particularly important for school leaders (73%), compared to other teachers (65%) and other educational staff (48%). The survey results are encouraging, as it appears that school leaders are considering, and hopefully modelling, how crucial maintaining a work-life balance is.

> I empathise with the obsession to stay one step ahead and the pressure of feeling that that's what's required of you at work. In order to feel worthy, I have the need to feel completely prepared at any given moment. Yet, in teaching, it has dawned on me that we can never achieve this—just like we can never achieve perfection, as discussed in Chapter 4.
>
> As a lecturer of trainee teachers, I am obliged and I have a duty to allow students time to reflect on work-life balance. I also think it's important for them to think about how they will achieve a balance between university, placement and personal time during their training and beyond. I heard once that a student (from a different university to mine) had been told by their school mentor to 'get used to not having a life, because that's what it's like to be a teacher!' I was horrified. Surely everyone is entitled to a life. I agree that student teachers need to have a realistic idea of the job of a teacher, but not by scaring them.
>
> Sadly though, some NQTs have bad experiences. An ex-student, who performed exceptionally well during every aspect of his PGCE training, still struggled in his NQT year. This was due to a huge lack of support from middle and senior management when he was trying to develop his teaching practice and manage a very challenging class. There was an enormous expectation for 'perfection' in his school, but with very little guidance for how to achieve it.
>
> Despite his efforts, he was unable to form productive working relationship with the teacher in the parallel year group and his support staff, who resented working with a young, male NQT. He faced a daily 'battle' of negative feelings towards him at school. In addition, he was working at least 60 hours a week to keep up with the demands and the changing policies of the school; after all, the expectations thrust upon him were to work in the evenings and at weekends.

> For over a term, he bottled up his worries, stresses and strains and tried to accept the level of pressure and severe anxiety he was feeling as 'normal' and part of the job. As a result, his mental health suffered, he lost his confidence for teaching and his enjoyment for the job.
>
> Eventually, he shared his feelings and gained support from his family and friends who reassured him and suggested that the school wasn't right for him. He resigned from his post a few days later. He was then offered a job at a small, village primary school and is now surrounded by extremely supportive colleagues. As a result, his love for teaching has returned. This is the advice he wanted to pass on:
>
> 'Avoid bottling your feelings up, do not accept that how you are feeling is okay and just the 'expectation of teaching'. Yes, the job is very hard and all-consuming, but it is not worth letting it impact onto your health. Make sure you are at the right school and that it suits you and supports you. The only way you can be the most effective teacher, and make a real difference to young people, is to make sure that you are okay first. Encourage your senior leadership team to put mental wellbeing of their staff (and children) first, and allow yourself to have time off, out of the classroom, where you can switch off from the pressure and rest.'

If your school expects you to be a workaholic, then it's time to escape or fight the misplaced logic of that expectation. The job will expand to fit the amount of time you are willing to devote to it, so beware. You could easily work 24 hours and still not get everything done, so prioritise, and then let go! Rath & Harter (2010) found that one's sense of pride increases with the hours worked, which explains the need in some people to continue working past the hours on their job description. In addition, they discuss how integral one's career is to our identity. A reminder of this in our society is when on first meeting someone, the initial question tends to be 'what do you do for a job?'

So, the message here is to aim to work smarter, rather than harder. The acronym 'SMART' stands for specific, measurable, attainable, relevant and time-limited. Make sure you realise and fulfil the purpose of each task that you carry out. Question the worth of everything you are asked to do (within limits). Don't be afraid to ask for help when you need it and to make your life easier and more manageable in any way you can. For example, explore the possibility of extra childcare (if you can afford it), or of employing a cleaner, especially if this creates an afternoon at the weekend for you to relax.

> When I returned to work, after the time I had needed off to recuperate, I made two key changes that made a massive difference to my wellbeing:
>
> - I was lucky because my father, after sensing my overwhelm, offered to pay for my three children to attend a local nursery for one day a week which was on one of the two days that I didn't work. This meant that I had free time to myself. Often, I caught up with jobs around the house or had a sleep in the day (which was a luxury).
> - My husband and I made an arrangement that we would each have one Saturday (until 6pm) per month off parenting duties. Having this time was liberating and precious and we both filled it with things that supported our wellbeing. I recall one Saturday, having a lie in, walking into town and sitting on the sunny window seat of a café eating a fried egg sandwich, sipping tea and reading a book; it felt like bliss. It was even a positive experience for me on the Saturday's where I was solely responsible for looking after the children. This was because I tended to plan ahead and sort out exciting things for us to do so I knew the children would be occupied. My husband, in comparison, would visit his parents and sit reading the newspaper while they occupied the children—what a cheat!

If you feel disillusioned about finding a school that has a clear focus on staff wellbeing, here are two examples of schools thinking outside of the box to ensure their staff have a work-life balance:

- One Headteacher managed to plan the timetable to allow the staff one afternoon off every week for them to do anything of their choice. Since starting this wellbeing initiative, he has seen an increase in productivity and a boost in morale.
- One school used a training day for a trip to Amsterdam. This proved a team-building exercise and meant that the staff could work together and explore museums and gather resources and ideas for a whole-school art project (although not all museums in Amsterdam may be suitable for school projects!). This exciting trip culminated in highly inspired staff and produced high-quality work from pupils.

Within the role of a teacher, inner conflicts or tensions can exist related to the time you devote to your work and home-life. If you work with children in an area of poverty or disadvantage, this conflict may feel even more pertinent and make you feel obligated to 'give your all.' Pillen et al. (2013:254) looked at the key tensions of new teachers, with one being:

> Wanting to invest time in a private life while feeling pressurized to commit time and energy to work.

A coping strategy they recommend for new teachers is to seek support from a significant other, usually a trusted mentor or colleague, to enable purposeful discussions, alongside searching for a solution themselves.

Tips towards a work-life balance

Here are a few suggestions of practical ways that you can stretch more personal time from your days ('STRETCH' is the acronym for remembering these):

Socialise

- Set up a variety of staff clubs to allow for socialisation at work and fit some fun pursuits into the working day; perhaps plan fitness or relaxation-focused activities such as Pilates or yoga. Ensure that you spend time enjoying the company of colleagues; don't isolate yourself. Work out which colleagues you can laugh, and moan, with. Sharing niggles and working through issues with other teachers creates a sense of solidarity and belonging. However, negativity should not dominate conversations.
- Having one member of staff to act as a Social Secretary may contribute to the organisation of social events amongst staff. For example, have a Friday breakfast together, where the Social Secretary collects the money and orders pancakes, muffins or bacon rolls from a local café delivered to the school. It's a bonus if the Headteacher fully support events like this and attends too.
- Maybe start regular 'Fika' times during lunchtimes. Fika is the Swedish concept of stopping for about 15 minutes and spending time with colleagues to stop, enjoy a hot drink and a small, sweet treat. Fika is a ritual that enables people to slow down, get in touch with the people around them and recharge their souls. Apparently, Ikea say that the best and

most productive ideas have arisen during Fika and, for this reason alone, management insist that all staff have two 12-minute periods of Fika each day.

> In 2000, at the school where I started my third year of teaching, there was an expectation that every Thursday night, staff left work at 4.15pm and retreated to the local pub. We didn't drink much, just a few glasses, but I recall the positive vibes and the camaraderie we shared. I noticed that as the years went by, the staff numbers going to the pub dwindled. The excuse was usually that they had too much work to catch up on. Sadly, by 2003, this pub tradition was no longer.
>
> For the past year at work, I have planned a Fika for university staff at least once a month. The idea is to familiarise staff with the practice of peer support so that they hopefully engage in it more in their own departments. I provide a signposting sheet for staff so that the mental health services for staff at my university are highlighted if anyone feels in crisis. We drink, eat, chat and sometimes play with Legos, do jigsaws, craft activities or play board games etc. The space exists at Fika to talk and share whatever is on our minds, and having that space cultivates peace and togetherness.

Teamwork

- Similarly, it helps to clawback time if you utilise the teamwork and support systems within in a school. Peer support can be used to boost morale, discuss ideas around wellbeing and to magpie the ideas of colleagues about how to achieve a work-life balance.
- Perhaps you could allocate each staff member a 'Wellbeing Buddy' who sends anonymous messages or gifts to keep a focus on wellbeing and valuing others. This can work like Secret Santa at Christmas and can inject some mystery and fun into work relationships as everyone tries to guess who their wellbeing buddy is.
- Bethune (2020) writes about 'kindness as an antidote to stress':

    It means that we need to look out for our colleagues and students more. Pay compliments, make cups of tea, hold doors open, show an interest in people's lives, and express concern and offer help when people are suffering. Schools that encourage care and concern for everyone in their community are less stressful places.

Rest

- Dedicate one day over the weekend to complete rest from work activities. I name this Sacred Saturday or Sacred Sunday.
- Aim to devote one hour to rest each day. Pick a time that suits you—mine was 7pm–8pm. You will need to plan this time into your day or it will evaporate and get consumed by something else. Remind yourself that you will not teach well if you are tired the next day and your body needs this time to recharge. Choose a different 'rest activity' each day, or the same one every day, if that suits you. Examples may include an aromatherapy bath, time to read a novel/magazine, meditation, listening to music, singing, applying a face pack or hair mask, lighting a candle and watching your favourite film etc.

Step 6: Adding more pleasurable pursuits to your life

Consider incorporating any of the ideas suggested below in Figure 3.1:

Examples of non-work activities to incorporate into your life to gain balance (A larger, colour version of this can be found on my website: www.supportingteacherwellbeing.wordpress.com)

Calming activities: Yoga, tai chi, meditation, mindfulness, aromatherapy baths, lighting a candle	Literacy-related activities: Gratitude diary, 'feeling good' log, scrap book, read something inspiring, email or write a letter, design a blog, look at some favourite photos	Creative activities: Crochet, knitting, colouring, sketching, baking, painting, sculpting	Musical activities: Singing, piano, guitar, listening to music, sound-bathing
Exercise: low and high intensity three times a week Walking, running, swimming, cycling, dance, gymnastics, visiting the gym, bowling, kayaking, golf	Social networks: Join a club, religious community, volunteering, spending time with friends, hug someone, join an online forum, Park Run	Connecting with nature: Woodland walks, gardening, fly a kite and watch the sky, orienteering, forest bathing, buy an allotment	Learn something new: Sign up to a local course or online training course, experiment with new recipes, learn a language
Animals/pet therapy: Dog walk, visit a zoo or safari park, volunteer at an animal shelter	Retail therapy: Shopping, window-shopping, online browsing, selling items online, flea markets, charity shops, car boot sales, antique shops	Decluttering: Declutter your house or classroom, do housework or tidying (known as 'dustercise'), organise your drawers	Alternative therapies: Massage, reflexology, acupuncture, aromatherapy
Time off: Book a holiday or weekend getaway to look forward to, do nothing, go to a retreat	Rest: Have a lie-in or pyjama day, sit on a lounger in the garden, take nano naps	Pampering activities: Wash your hair, give yourself a facial or face-pack, soak your feet in a foot-spa, go on a spa day, have a beauty treatment	Eating: Go to a café or restaurant and treat yourself to a lovely meal, cook your favourite foods, do some juicing, make smoothies, soups etc (chopping can relieve depression)
Entertainment: Watch a comedy film or programme and laugh, visit the theatre or cinema, sporting event	Invigorating activities: Body brushing or exfoliating, drink hot lemon	Trips: Visit the beach and look out to sea, travel on the train, visit a distant relative	Family-inspired activities: Treasure hunts, geocaching, jigsaws, family quizzes

Figure 3.1 A collection of non-work activities: Ideas to help maintain a work-life balance.

Email

- Decide as a staff not to answer emails out of office hours and on weekends. Also, make it clear that the expectation in your school is that there is at least five working days grace (or whatever you decide as a school for this) to answer emails, except under exceptional circumstances. Having email notifications set up explaining not to expect an immediate response should lessen the pressure on teachers.
- It should not be encouraged that staff access their emails via their mobile phones so that when they are at home, work cannot interfere and encroach on personal time.

Time

- Consider doing an audit of your time over one typical week.

Step 7: Audit your time

- Use this audit in staff meetings when discussing work-life balance. The audit results may illuminate where change is needed most urgently. For example, if much time is spent by the majority of staff in a school on administrative tasks, then the following week an audit could be undertaken to look at what administrative tasks are being done in a week. Once completed and compared, questions may arise about whether any tasks could be simplified, aborted or carried about by admin or support staff instead. It may be useful to reflect upon which parts of a teacher's job is negotiable and which they have no control over. The drawback is the time being taken to complete the audit, but this is necessary if change is to happen at a whole-school level and in the best way for your school.
- If audits are completed but then nothing changes, this could result in the disillusionment of staff. Therefore, audits need to have meaning and aim to invoke change. Alternatively, you could complete an audit on how you spend your personal time against how much time you devote to your job. Changes could also be instigated for these results, for example, saving time by having groceries delivered to your house rather than going out to shop or delegating jobs to your teenage children to free up some time for you etc.

- To gain some time for personal pursuits, leave early from school once a week on the same day. I suggest Wednesdays so that you get a 'mini-weekend' in the middle of the week. This does require planning though, so that on Tuesday you are prepped ready for Thursday. This will allow you to have a complete break from everything work-related on a Wednesday night.
- Set a leaving time each day for yourself and don't deviate from it. Do what you can up until that time, and then leave. If you must, set a timer so you have no excuse for missing this self-imposed clock-out time.
- Consider sharing the travelling to work with a colleague if you live nearby. This can work to save time if you are able to travel with a colleague that you plan with (for example, a parallel year-group class). It also serves to make the journey less stressful if you can be a passenger for half the week, rather than driving through the traffic on your own.
- If you are obligated to do an after-school club at your school, then pick one wisely and choose something that you enjoy doing so the time is spent positively.

> I volunteered to run a Film Club that was very popular and allowed me to mark books while I supervised a room of quiet children, which was a win-win. The local supermarket donated popcorn and the school paid for some juice cartons, so there was no tidying up afterwards. I also ran a mindfulness club, which allowed me to switch off and benefit from the quiet this provoked. I bought 10 cheap fleece blankets and donated the old cushions from my home to the club so that children were warm and comfortable when meditating (after all, this was a good excuse to treat myself to some new cushions at home, which was very good for my wellbeing!)

Challenge workload

- Reflect upon all the jobs that you undertake and, if you don't see purpose, don't do them, especially if they have no relevance to pupil progress. Don't be afraid to question school leaders, diplomatically, about the reasons why you are being asked to do something. If the reason seems pointless, then suggest alternative practices that may make more sense and exert less pressure on staff.

> Writing onerous reports for parents, three times a year, was one example of a practice I always felt was a waste of my time. In my school, staff respectfully probed into the justification of reports and they were then limited to twice a year. In addition, the written amount was decreased by the use of checklists rather than narrative.

- Say no to extra responsibility. Only say yes to extra responsibility if you will personally gain from it and you are passionate about the work involved. Only agree to performance-management targets that you are motivated to fulfil.
- Only mark work if it is meaningful, has a purpose and supports pupil progress. You will obviously need to refer to your school's marking policy, but enquire as to whether you can put your own stamp on this (maybe literally use stamps or stickers for a 'well done for…' comment, instead of hand writing all the feedback). Follow the three M's for marking, so only mark work if the process is 'meaningful, manageable and motivating,' (DfE, 2017, Reducing Workload poster—see Useful resources).
- A great tip is to ask pupils to stack their books open on the page you need to mark which saves you from flicking through every book to find the right page. Encourage peer and self-assessment, if it fits with the lesson, so that you can limit your marking each day. Use verbal feedback as a marking tool as much as you can.

Holiday

- Book a holiday or weekend retreat: Book in advance so you can look forward to it and get a little thrill thinking about it on tiring and hectic days. Safeguard your holidays and protect what's important to you.

Perhaps one of the common practices of a teacher that disrupts and encroaches on your personal time is planning. So, here's some tips on how to plan effectively but by saving time.

Work-life balance—Planning

Overplanning for lessons is a sure-fire way to lose your work-life balance. Your school will have set ways for you to undertake long-term and medium-term planning, but short-term planning, in many schools, is dependent on the individual. It is crucial that you do not spend too long on meaningless planning but use the best format for you.

On the 'Reducing Teacher Workload' poster (DfE, 2019) it states to:

> Give lesson plans the proportionate status they merit, and no more, to lessen teacher workload.

The only time that you may wish to overplan for a lesson is when you are being observed.

My advice is to adapt and use high-quality online lessons plans, for example, those from Hamilton Trust (see Useful resources). Indeed, Hamilton Trust was specifically founded by a campaign called 'Save our Sundays for teachers' to encourage teachers to gain back precious weekend time formally spent on onerous planning.

I couldn't blame my school for my lack of balance, but I could certainly blame myself! I recall striving to be 100% resourced for a lesson and under pressure to have considered every eventuality. With time, however, I began to have a more 'good enough' approach to my teaching and preparation and morphed into a more relaxed, spontaneous and child-centred practitioner.

Eventually, I came up with an answer to keep me sane. I read about a bridge in America that takes so long to maintain that when the workers have finished painting it, it is time to start all over again. I developed the acceptance that I will never get to the end of my job-list. I managed to make peace with this and begin to focus on enjoying the process instead.

On a more practical note, I found it helpful to thoroughly plan one lesson a day (mainly rotating between the core subjects of Maths, English and Science and other subjects too); let's call it my 'focus lesson.' This meant I felt like I had gone 'above and beyond' having poured energy and thought into the resources and delivery for that one lesson. This stopped the nagging feelings of guilt that I hadn't prepared enough. I would then plan two other lessons per day (another core lesson and a foundation subject lesson) to a 'good enough' standard. My main assessment, and therefore my marking, would be linked to my focus lesson, which I tended to teach first thing each day when I was fresh. Teaching this lesson first also meant that there was the most opportunity for me (or my lovely TA) to mark during the day so that I could avoid staying late at school to mark. I took the pupil's 'Big Writing' books home on a Monday night, but never marked at home on any other night. The majority of my planning occurred on my PPA (planning, preparation and assessment) afternoon, which was when I created my five focus lessons for the following week. The pressure was off me then, during the weekends, as I only needed to do a 'good enough' job on the planning for the remaining lessons for that week, which often consisted of lessons that I had previously taught, so all they needed were a few tweaks to suit the individual pupils' needs in my current class. This method worked for me, but it may not for you. Every teacher needs to find the structure and strategies that work for them and their particular school ethos.

If you find that you need a short-term planning strategy that will save you time, feel free to use this one, which worked superbly for me, but (as I've said countless times already in this book—sorry, I'm like a stuck record) this may not personally work for you...

I called this child-centred planning format the Path of Progress (POP). Here is an example of what a Year 1 maths lesson on symmetry looked like to the children displayed on the classroom Interactive Whiteboard (see Figure 3.2) and what my teacher/TA planning sheet looked like, too (see Figure 3.3) (These figures can be found on my website).

I adapted the Path of Progress from the idea of a learning journey. It is a visual representation of a journey to achieve the learning objective (arriving at the castle) whilst visiting various success criteria (shown as the landmarks: a house, tiger, tree and lake). The 'secret room' is an extension activity planned for those that have achieved the learning objective within the lesson. This format allows for flexibility and differentiation, for example, children may not visit every landmark or may achieve

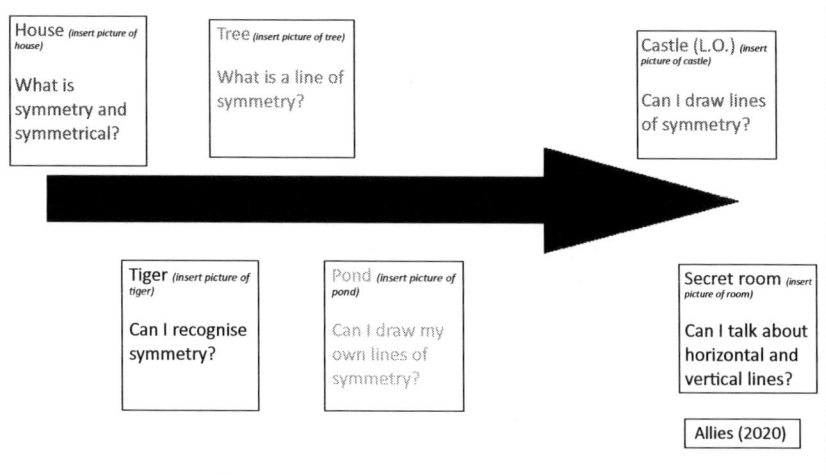

House *(insert picture of house)* What is symmetry and symmetrical?	Tree *(insert picture of tree)* What is a line of symmetry?		Castle (L.O.) *(insert picture of castle)* Can I draw lines of symmetry?
	Tiger *(insert picture of tiger)* Can I recognise symmetry?	Pond *(insert picture of pond)* Can I draw my own lines of symmetry?	Secret room *(insert picture of room)* Can I talk about horizontal and vertical lines?
			Allies (2020)

Figure 3.2 My Path of Progress (POP): Symmetry-Year 1.

78 STRATEGIES FOR WELLBEING

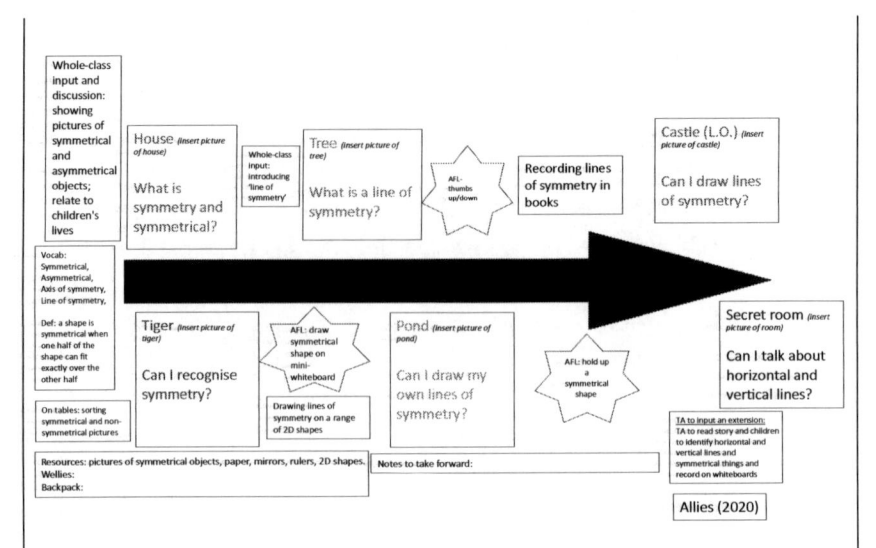

Figure 3.3 My Path of Progress (POP): Symmetry-Year 1.

each one quickly and move on at different paces. There are 'assessment for learning' opportunities at various stages.

The value of this planning format to me was that it encouraged autonomy as the children were fully involved in their own learning. Occasionally, I would leave the learning objective as a mystery so they could work out what they thought it was from looking at the success criteria. I would also (once they got used to this format) only give them the learning objective and they would draw their 'journey' on a mini whiteboard, including ideas for each success criteria. This process encouraged the children to use metacognition as they developed an understanding and awareness of their thought processes, their own learning patterns and the art of problem-solving.

You may be wondering why it says 'wellies' and 'backpack' at the bottom of the page. I had a large laminated picture of Wellington boots displayed on one wall of my classroom, and another of a big backpack. During each lesson, children would record in words or pictures what they were 'stuck on' (using the metaphor of being stuck in the mud during a journey). We had a whole-class discussion where these ideas were shared during the lesson's plenary. In contrast, the backpack was used for pupils to record what helped them and aided their learning on the journey. Often, children recorded the names of their peers or classroom resources. They sometimes even drew a picture of the TA or myself and we could question them about how and why we help them—it always proves entertaining to see a picture of yourself drawn by a six-year-old!

The workload of teachers

According to the National Foundation for Educational Research think tank (2019), teachers experience higher levels of job-related stress than any other professionals. They explained that because work is so intensive during term times, this often leads to a poorer work-life balance and higher stress levels. Dealing with paperwork is a great source of discontent, as teaching can evolve into a string of unmanageable, unrealistic tasks. Indeed, in 2014, the Teacher and Workload Survey Report by the National Union of Teachers (NUT) found that 96% of teachers said that workload has a negative effect on their life.

Dr Bousted (2019) of the National Education Union (NEU) commented that

> When faced with impossible workloads, endless accountability, a testing culture run riot and flat or underfunded pay deals year after year, it is all too common for good teachers to leave the profession.

It's clear that we need a major focus in the UK upon teacher workload. The Organisation for Economic Co-operation and Development (OECD) exposed that only teachers in Japan and Singapore work longer hours than those in Britain; Fujita (1997) found that most Japanese teachers devote up to 12 hours a day in school, with many leaving their school at 8pm.

The Reducing Teacher Workload teacher-led review group (DfE, 2017, see Useful resources) shared the following recommendations about marking and planning:

- 'Marking practice that does not have the desired impact on pupil outcomes is a time-wasting burden for teachers that has to stop'
- 'Teachers should not be spending their time on bureaucracy that does not add value. Teachers' time should be protected and used to make a difference.'

Unfortunately, I fear that the application of the proposed initiatives from the DfE (2019), such as to design 'a programme of work to tackle workload and improve wellbeing' in a school, would ironically add enormously to a teacher's workload! Although, I imagine that you feel similarly about some of the actions I propose within this book! I recommend involving the administrative staff of your school to minute meetings and communicate what was discussed so the burden does not fall to school leaders.

Workload procrastination

Procrastination is common. If you struggle with this and it has become a habit, then you are not alone. Steele (2012) found that 95% of people admit to procrastinating at some point in their lives.

I know that I procrastinated a lot while writing this book, and there were times when I felt a pull towards even doing housework instead of writing (and doing housework is not like me!). I certainly relate to what Fiore has to say about the reasons why we procrastinate below...

People 'procrastinate because it makes sense, given how vulnerable they feel to criticism, failure and their own perfectionism.' (Fiore, 2007:3).

Often procrastination is attributed to laziness, but Fiore writes that it happens in:

> an attempt to resolve a variety of underlying issues, including low self-esteem, perfectionism, fear of failure and of success, indecisiveness, an imbalance between work and play, ineffective goal setting and negative concepts about work and yourself.
>
> (2007:4–5).

If you are prone to procrastination, then first-off, it is important to be aware and consciously recognise that you are procrastinating. Secondly, you need to identify the reasons that underpin this behaviour. Think back to times when you have put things off and ask yourself how and why you avoided them. You are a fabulous professional so think 'FAB PRO' as the acronym to remember the following tips to avoid procrastination:

Forgive

- In order to limit the chance of you procrastinating again, you need to forgive yourself for previous times when you have done it.

Avoid distractions

- Avoid distractions, unless you are completing a low-concentration task where having some background noise will help.
- Telling someone when you intend to do a task may help you persevere rather than distracting yourself.
- Avoid exaggerating the tasks that are hanging over you as a distraction technique. Ask yourself if you are inflating how important a task is or the time that is needed to undertake it.

Build in breaks

- Break jobs down into manageable chunks.
  A friend of mine once quoted Desmond Tutu to me at a time when I when I was overwhelmed with my workload, and this has stayed with me: 'There is only one way to eat an elephant, a bite at a time.'
- Try the Pomodoro technique (Cirillo, n.d.), which involves using a timer to break down jobs into 30-minute intervals separated by short breaks. If you work for too long, your productivity dips, and the breaks will improve your mental agility (Ericsson, 1990).

Prioritise

- As much as possible, tackle a task as soon as it is given to you rather than letting jobs build up. Deal with the task that you know is the most important first. Many teachers find that prioritising their workload using an approach such as ABC helps them. The A is for urgent, B is for important and C is for things that can wait. Plan your work in accordance with your energy highs and lows; ask yourself if you are you a morning lark or a night owl. I'm not sure what to call someone who has the most energy in the afternoon, though?
- Get the tasks that you know you will find the least pleasant out of the way early in the day. Alternatively, using the Eisenhower method of prioritisation may help. Mulder (2017) writes about how about you should deal with each of these categories (her advice is in BOLD below). The Eisenhower method of procrastination is when you categorise tasks into:

- important/urgent (e.g. child protection or safeguarding issues) **DO**
- not important/urgent (e.g. time-dependent paperwork) **DELEGATE**
- not urgent/important (e.g. planning for next week) **SCHEDULE**
- or not urgent/not important (e.g. unnecessary marking) **ELIMINATE**

- Create only realistic to-do lists, and allocate a time limit to each task and keep to it. Remember the value in completing some things to a 'good enough' standard.

Reward

- Reward yourself when you have completed a task.

> *I am experimenting with ways to do this that don't involve food. For example, yesterday I finished responding to all the emails that had mounted up in my inbox and then treated myself to a relaxing bath.*

- Recall the good feeling that you get when you accomplish a task and use this to drive you forward. Empower yourself by owning the task you complete and accept that you are in control. Try to find ways to appreciate and enjoy the journey of doing the task rather than feeling like you can only enjoy yourself when it is finished.

Organise well

- Consider using a free self-organisation app, such as Trello, where you can create cards with comments, files attached and checklists with due dates etc.

Useful resources

- The DfE, 'Reducing workload: Supporting teachers in the early stages of their career: Advise for school leaders, induction tutors, mentors and appropriate bodies' (March 2019) report may prove informative and

- can be found at: https://assets.publishing.service.gov.uk/government/uploads/system/uploads/attachment_data/file/786178/Advice_for_ECTs_update.pdf
- Consider joining The Chartered College of Teaching, who issue an annual publication called 'The Profession'. The 2018 issue has an article on supporting your workload as an early career teacher.
- The DfE designed a workload myth-busting poster which can be found at: https://assets.publishing.service.gov.uk/government/uploads/system/uploads/attachment_data/file/593913/6.2799_DFE_MB_Reducing_Teacher_Workload_Poster_20161213_print.pdf
- Here you will find the DfE (2018) workload toolkits: https://www.gov.uk/guidance/school-workload-reduction-toolkit
- For high-quality online lessons plans from Hamilton Trust for you to adapt, please visit: https://www.hamilton-trust.org.uk/

Takeaway message: Do the best teachers work the longest hours?

It might be a common mindset for teachers to think that if they are not stressed and extremely busy at school, then they are not working hard enough. Some colleagues might extenuate the hours they have worked and equate this with virtue. One of the problems in our modern society is that our culture can sometimes reward overwork, and even anxious behaviour, and then, if support is lacking, this can lead to ill health. Highly anxious teachers may experience self-denigration for not coping better with work demands. Depression is often stigmatised, but, in contrast, is often seen as more of a legitimate mental health illness than anxiety. More about coping with anxiety and depression next...

4

WHAT OTHER STRATEGIES SUPPORT TEACHER WELLBEING?

Dealing with anxiety and depression at school

Primarily, it is crucial that you look out for signs of anxiety and depression in yourself and other colleagues. Again, I refer you back to the mental health continuum model for teachers (Figure 2.1). It's crucial that even mild symptoms of anxiety or depression are dealt with before they develop into moments of crisis or burnout. I recall a story from the BBC News (2019) that illustrates how desperate one teacher felt; she considered driving her car into a tree to avoid going back to the classroom. The Hampshire teacher wanted to remain anonymous but had a desire to speak out to raise awareness about the levels of stress in the teaching profession. She explained how difficult it was for her to recognise her depression or share her feelings:

> I could literally feel myself drowning, but I couldn't express it, I couldn't tell anyone. I felt ashamed.

Advice for teachers and school leaders about supporting or coping with severe depression and anxiety is covered in Chapter 6, but here are some simple strategies to allow you to feel more in control of your mild anxiety or depression. Think of the acronym 'SATS' to recall the following tips, which is a word you will be familiar with already I imagine:

Share your feelings

Rogers (2012:68) wrote that sharing worries with a trusted colleague can:

> help to articulate, define and delineate the shape and boundaries of the things we've been worrying about. We then need to take necessary, reasonable and possible action.

It seems crucial to recognise what we can change, which is how we feel about the situation and our response to problems. If anxious or depressive thoughts are creating a viscous circle for you so you feel powerless to do anything, then hopefully talking through your anxieties with someone will be enlightening. It may allow you to gain an alternative perspective and some distance from your worries momentarily, which should offer some relief.

Ask for help

If your anxiety or depression is stopping you from working to the best of your ability, similar to having a physical illness, you might ask school leaders for support. If your mental health has become unmanageable, it may be possible for you to have a few days at home to recuperate. The website WeAreTeachers.com (2019) wrote about how the notion of taking a 'mental health day' began. It was when an email to a boss appeared on Twitter that said,

> I'm taking today and tomorrow to focus on my mental health. Hopefully I'll be back next week refreshed and back to 100%.

Of course, it would not be fair to take a kind and compassionate school leader for granted, though, by asking for time off when it is not needed.

However, if you feel you are truly suffering, then it might be worth requesting some time off, especially if you feel your low mental health is affecting your pupils. However, this time must be spent wisely; you need to invest this time to put strategies in place to face your mental health needs to allow you to remain at work. The idea of teachers taking a 'mental health day' is likely to be controversial, but it would be nice to think that we can get to a stage where the mental health of employees is such an important issue that ideas like this are considered and the parity is acknowledged between physical and mental health. My only concern would be how 'mental health days' could be managed in practical terms, without adding stress to other workers or school leaders.

Try to understand

It may be useful for you to uncover the underpinning reasons for your anxiety or depression (this is Step 4). Often these justifications and concerns relate to the past or the future. I wonder if you agree with the following quote about our human experience:

> If you are depressed, you are living in the past. If you are anxious, you are living in the future. If you are at peace, you are living in the moment
>
> (Lao Tzu, 2018).

If this rings true for you, you may wish to read my section on mindfulness (later in this chapter) and see if there is value in incorporating a few strategies to bring your focus back to the present moment during the day. It is interesting to reflect on the fact that animals don't experience full-blown anxiety due to their inability to conceptualise the future. They may experience a stress-response (and you know all about that from Chapter 2), but their trigger is only fear in the moment, therefore their anxiety is often short-lived.

Stay organised and 'let go'

Routines and planning ahead often make people feel safe and secure. It may help to limit your decisions so you can save your energy for other things, for example, by developing daily routines, such as always having fish for tea on a Thursday. These rituals may save you from making unnecessary choices and limit your anxious feelings. Kondo (2014) encourages us to minimise our belongings and to only keep the objects, at home or work, that make us feel joy or have a practical use.

In our modern society, many of us tend to be searching for happiness outside of ourselves in external gratification and in the grasping of material possessions rather than looking inwards, where comfort truly lies. The term 'FOMO' is being used for the common fear of missing out. However, there is a lot to be said for simplifying or decluttering your life and 'letting go' of what other people have or are experiencing. It is tempting to use social media, but when it becomes an obsession or you are spending valuable time on it, then perhaps it is time to realise that it is not serving your wellbeing. Hunt et al. (2018) found that limiting your social media usage to 30 minutes a day may increase wellbeing levels. It is honourable to celebrate other people's achievements, but what you see on social media may not be reality. We need to apply a critical approach to what we read online. Without this criticality, social media may be making you feel lacking and inferior. Limiting the time that you spend on social media may be one adjustment you can make that lessens anxiety or depression and elevates your self-esteem.

Self-esteem and confidence

Self-esteem can be defined as:

> belief and confidence in your own ability and value (Cambridge Dictionary).

Those teachers with high self-esteem will generally be more able to deal with stress in school than those with low self-esteem. If a teacher's self-esteem is high, then they can develop a positive sense of 'identity, security and belonging' (Coppersmith, 1967 cited in Rogers, 1992). But how do you achieve high self-esteem if you are feeling devalued and your efforts as a teacher are being unrecognised?

Even though Rogers wrote about his concern for teachers back in 1992, the same issues he identified then are still prevalent and widespread today.

Rogers (1992:3) detailed his concern for the low morale so many teachers experience whilst dealing with the 'physical, psychological and spiritual wear and tear related to their job.' Rogers (1992:5) also wrote about how significant our jobs can be in shaping our self-worth:

> ...the way we think about ourselves affects how we feel and, consequently, how we behave in our jobs, how we relate to others, how motivated we are, how confidently we can address our roles as teachers...While it is legitimate to state our needs with appropriate assertion, we will feel worse and have less esteem for ourselves if we rely and depend on others to create our worth as a person.

Self-esteem ultimately comes from within the person concerned but can be helped along by encouragement, affirmation, positivity and the feeling of being valued by others (more specifically the government, school leaders and colleagues). Self-esteem is not fixed and with resilience and the strong will to battle a negative mindset, it can be possible to increase self-esteem, especially with the support of others. Indeed, Rogers (2012:27) states:

> Colleague support is the crucial anchor variable in addressing stress of any sort in our profession.

This section on self-esteem resonates with me, as I find it difficult to celebrate my achievements and tend to focus upon the negative aspects of myself, which can lead to low self-worth and feelings of inadequacy about my ability as a teacher. This may be due to circumstances related to my family life growing up. I tend to have little confidence in my own opinion, especially in confrontational situations. I once found support from a colleague that I didn't know particularly well. She provided me with empathy and understanding on a difficult day, which was most welcome and unexpected...

I had been teaching for about 10 years when I had a class with a handful of parents who appeared to strive to make my job difficult (or that's how I perceived it at the time). I was part of a job-share class and my job-share partner needed time off work due to her pregnancy. I was asked to cover her days and agreed to do this specifically to maintain consistency for the class. There was a child in the class that struggled with his behaviour on the playground, and a few incidents arose where he was accused of bullying and engaging in rough play with his friends. I asked to meet with his parents to discuss his behaviour openly and to suggest how we could work together to improve his behaviour.

From the start of the meeting, the parents were defensive and would not entertain the fact that their son had behaved inappropriately at school. They informed me that his behaviour was due to my inability to manage the behaviour of all the children on my own without my job-share partner. The parents left this meeting incensed and posted some hateful comments on Facebook about me as a teacher. Sadly, other parents who were friends with them added various defamatory remarks to the post too, for example, complaining about a day when I had forgotten to ask their child to change their reading book (what a crime!). The next day, the mother I had met with was so angry that she gathered four other mothers who came in a group to confront me. This was daunting and scary, and I was caught off-guard at the end of the school day when I was in the classroom alone. Thankfully, a colleague heard the raised voices of the parents and knocked on the door. I looked visibly shaken and so my colleague explained that I was needed in a meeting (little white lie). The presence of another member of staff seemed to diffuse the anger of the parents. To end the 'discussion', although it would have been better described as an 'attack', I proposed to meet with every parent the next day. I also added that I felt that it was unfair to speak about the personal details of everyone's complaints in a group and so meeting individually would be fairer. Having my colleague there gave me courage to speak up for myself.

When the parents left, my colleague sat and listened patiently to what had happened and told me that I did not deserve that treatment. She told me that I was a very able teacher and that the school and my class were lucky to have me, especially as I was covering for my absent job-share partner. She told me that my bubbly and friendly personality often lifted her spirits; I was the joker of the staffroom. If I had not had the chance to debrief with this colleague, I hate to think of where my negative ruminations would have taken me that night. Rather, I felt proud of myself for handling this situation calmly and made a promise that I would not blame or berate myself internally, which was what I usually did. As a child, I had been taught to consider the other person's view as more important and worthy than mine in any argument or altercation, so this had become habitual for me. I pushed that inner voice away and tried to remember the soothing words of my colleague, which helped enormously.

The following day, I spoke with the mother who I had originally met with. What followed was a positive end to this story. Instead of showing her the frustration and resentment I felt towards her, especially due to the Facebook post (which hopefully today would

> be dealt with by leaders in schools), I empathised with her. I believe this was due to the way my colleague had boosted my self-esteem the day before by validating positive aspects of my persona. I explained to the mother that I could see how much she cared for her son and that I could understand how difficult it must be for her to hear about his playground behaviour. I asked her about how he behaved at home. She admitted that she felt overwhelmed with the violent fights her son had with his brother. She began crying and sharing details of the troubled time she had had at primary school and indeed in her own educational experiences as a child. She felt that she had been treated unfairly by teachers and had always vowed to protect her own children from going through anything similar. I began to realise that her anger had little to do with my ability as a teacher and more to do with this mother's attitude about teachers generally based upon her history.

The Mental Health Foundation (n.d: 21) acknowledges that:

> it can be tempting to invest everything in building self-esteem around work success. That often means that people with mental health problems give everything at work and are high achievers. It also creates a risk that when things go wrong, when mistakes are made, or when change is necessary, people may take it personally.

Here are some tips, therefore, to build confidence in order to minimise this risk (I couldn't make an acronym for this one...):

Focus on the positives

- Make a list of your positive aspects and ask your closest colleague to add to these. Keep the list somewhere so you can remind yourself of your strengths and positive attributes. By reflecting on your teaching strengths and celebrating them, you build a personal sense of self-worth and belief, which ultimately leads to confidence. This would make a constructive, self-affirmative and bonding exercise to complete at the end or beginning of a staff meeting. Pieces of paper with every staff's name on the top could be passed around the table for everyone to add an anonymous positive characteristic, although handwriting may need to be disguised to maintain anonymity.

- If this seems too cheesy an idea, then it might be a rewarding experience to have a sheet with 'Staff Shout Out' on the staffroom wall so that staff can add Post-It notes with positive comments about colleagues. This can be added to over a few weeks and is a chance to celebrate each other and induce a grateful spirit.

> I once encouraged a Year 4 class to complete the former of the exercises above with their peers in a PSHE lesson on the first day of a new academic year (Later, I briefly discuss the value of PSHE in aiding the positive mental health of your class). Anyway, each pupil had a card with their name on it, which was passed around the class and everyone wrote a word that described that person on it until all the cards had been circulated. I remember one child's face lighting up when she read her card at the end of the task. I recall that she had previously struggled with low confidence and that she seemed to blossom during the academic year I taught her. Of course, I have no proof that this was as a result of this class exercise, but I noticed that she kept this card in her tray all year and a few times I caught her looking at it. I would like to think that the time I spent on PSHE had a momentous effect on her self-esteem, but that would be arrogant of me. There are a whole host of reasons that could contribute to her increase in confidence that year.

Live by your values

- Remind yourself of your strong values and the reasons why you chose to become a teacher. Confidence begins inside of yourself and is driven by these values and self-beliefs. Allow these reasons and your identity to manifest as values that run through every decision you make. Don't underestimate the difference that you are making as a teacher and the power you possess to do good in the classroom. I regularly interview candidates for Initial Teacher Training (ITT) courses, and when the candidates are asked why they have chosen teaching as a career, they usually mention a special teacher that has had a profound and memorable impact on them. Every day, I recommend that you think about what you wish to be remembered for and the impact that you will undoubtedly have on the next generation. Ask yourself, how would you like to be described by the children in your class?
- Incidentally, a talking therapy called Acceptance Commitment Therapy (ACT) focuses on celebrating positive aspects like living your life in

accordance with your values. ACT encourages you to make life decisions after reflecting upon what is meaningful and true for you only, rather than measuring your worth against anything else.

Be prepared and have fun

- Stay well-prepared for lessons and entertain yourself by incorporating inventive, interactive and humorous elements into your lessons.
- Appreciate the level of freedom that you are given and have faith that you know your learners well enough to choose novel and engaging ways to address learning objectives. By showing enthusiasm and a love for each subject, you will translate this passion to children.
- After a lesson, ask for feedback from your pupils about what they have learnt and if, and why, they enjoyed it. Consult with your teaching assistant to find out what they thought were the highlights of lessons. Your self-esteem will be boosted from listening to the positive remarks. If you receive any worthwhile negative feedback, then use this as a tool for change.

> I get a buzz and boost from the anticipation of a lesson that I am excited about teaching when I know it is well thought out and interesting. An example of this is a session I plan when teaching art to trainee teachers; it involves children's picture books. I design the lesson so that the first half is focusing on one illustrator of children's books, the lovely Petr Horacek. We watch clips of Petr drawing, find out what inspired him and marvel over a range of his books. As Petr was born in Prague in the Czech Republic, I insinuate that he still lives abroad, so you can imagine the student's faces when there is a knock on the door during the second half of the lesson and Petr walks into the room! Over the years, I receive emails from the students thanking me for this lesson and this has boosted my confidence. Examples of these comments include: 'you honestly made me feel like a child again. It really inspired me and gave me a different look on teaching as a whole'; 'What you did today was over and above an art lesson. You are a role model we all aspire to be like.' Seems like I'm blowing my own trumpet here, but I think it is important that we get better at shouting about the things we accomplish and celebrating the things that go well.

Do power poses

- Research, such as Carney et al. (2019), has found that doing power poses before teaching can have a dramatic effect upon your self-confidence. Carney et al.'s study found that cortisol (the stress hormone) decreased significantly after their participants did brief power poses before a performance.

> I admit to doing some power poses in the toilet before a presentation that I was nervous about. It did seem to work, as usually I am prone to shaky hands when I'm apprehensive, but I didn't have them on this occasion.

Be decisive and consistent when managing behaviour

- If you are firm but fair and keep your cool when managing behaviour, demonstrating your confidence in your ability, this will result in the children having confidence in you.
- One of the most frequent ways that teacher confidence is eroded is by a class that simply refuses to listen. If your class displays continual examples of low-level disruption, then this is likely to wear you down. Don't ever shout over the noise of a class. Instead practice standing and waiting completely calmly and quietly (no matter how you're feeling inside). You'll be amazed by what a powerful tool silence is and how it commands instant respect.
- Have a set of realistic and clear rules that have been suggested and approved by pupils, and stick to these consistently.

Develop in self-efficacy

- Only when teachers show increased belief in their capabilities will there be less blame in the system; higher self-efficacy among teachers could enable a move towards a more autonomous way of being for teachers. We need to take responsibility as active participants, as well as expecting respect and care from our employers.

I'll get off my soapbox now and discuss another internal conflict we may have as a teacher—the battle for perfection. On not achieving it, we might berate ourselves and then our self-esteem could suffer. By ending perfectionism in yourself, you can strive for increased wellbeing.

Perfectionism

I found this section difficult to write, ironically due to my perfectionist tendencies! I wrote and rewrote the beginning paragraph (below) many times over. It was hard to block out the negative self-talk in my head saying that I'm not 'good enough', or academic enough, to be writing a book at all, but I got there in the end…

You may not agree with me, but I wished to include this topic as, in my experience, many teachers are perfectionists. Perfectionism can work against a teacher, creating a negative cycle of self-criticism and self-worth. In a caring profession like teaching, it is easy to become a perfectionist, as you want to do the very best for children in your care. Some workplaces add to this perfectionist drive and perpetuate the message that unreasonable tasks are expected, for example, finishing very extensive reports in a short period of time. Teachers may strive for exceptionally high standards of performance and place great emphasis on someone's evaluation of their behaviour. I worry that this negatively effects a teacher's wellbeing as they strive to attain a level of perfectionism that is unobtainable and unrealistic. I imagine that the pressure a perfectionist teacher experiences when being observed can result in excessive stress, like I experienced here…

> *There is a part of me that thrives under the pressure of having a lesson of mine observed. However, I assert enormous pressure on myself to 'perform' to the best of my ability. As a born 'show-off', I'll admit that the part of teaching that I enjoy is being centre stage. However, in recent years the 'all-singing and all-dancing' lessons of old that used to be deemed as 'outstanding' are, quite rightly, out of date. I agree now that the best lessons aren't all about a teachers' 'performance' but are all to do with the children's learning and how a teacher facilitates progress. Indeed, I observe many, in my eyes, 'outstanding' lessons from teachers that are admittedly introverted, unassuming characters and are not interested in putting on a show but just focus entirely on the essential outcomes and pupils' needs.*

> *Anyway, I have always strived to be judged as an 'outstanding' teacher and have only once achieved this label—my first ever Ofsted grading in 1999—and it was for one of my 'full of myself as a teacher' displays. Now, looking back, I can recall the great lengths I went to to teach the 'perfect' lesson. For instance, the over-the-top lesson plans that I produced for the inspectors even had learning objectives for the children's visits to the toilet. Moreover, the lesson Ofsted observed took blood, sweat and tears to create and more time than would ever be realistic to prepare for a lesson normally. Nonetheless, the crucial aspect for me was that I was being as perfect as humanly possible, and unfortunately for me, once I had I attained 'outstanding', I felt under pressure to keep this up. To this day, I have not achieved this, at least not by some 'official' arbitrary judgement.*
>
> *My Headteacher at the school I taught at for 16 years graded me 'good' or 'good with outstanding' over the years, but never solely 'outstanding'. This stung and left me feeling inadequate. This seems ridiculous, as I wasn't being graded as 'requires improvement' like some teachers have to bounce back from. I recall one lesson observation morning where I even crashed my car on the way to school; while driving, I had been distractedly rehearsing the lesson in my head. As it turned out during that fateful observation, which cost me my no-claims bonus, one child had been absentmindedly staring out of the window. The Headteacher noticed the daydreaming child while I inputted the most significant learning points, therefore my lesson feedback was that she was off-task and disengaged during a crucial part of the lesson. I failed to notice, and address this, hence my Headteacher's grade that day of 'good'. And, do you think I was happy with 'good'? Of course not. The Headteacher explained that I could not be deemed as 'outstanding' because there was one child who had not shown evidence of making progress. There was no opportunity for me to share that this child's parents were in the process of divorcing and therefore may have been the reason for her disengaged manner. Anyway, my overriding memory of this lesson observation was walking home that night deflated and disappointed with myself.*

An analysis of my perfectionism here would suggest that the following process may be at play (according to what I've read):

1) Having once taught the perfect 'outstanding' lesson, many moons ago, I was rewarded by a rush of dopamine (the 'feel-good' or 'reward' chemical), which gave me a powerful feeling of success.

2) Because these powerful feelings only occurred once and were memorable, then, as a perfectionist, I have chased a repeat of this perfect lesson relentlessly. The release of dopamine motivates an individual to seek out more and more pleasurable rewards. I also have an addictive personality!

3) Having not ever achieved this 'outstanding' label again, my self-worth has decreased and I have felt a failure in many respects, especially when I hear of other teachers being graded as 'outstanding'. Comparing yourself to others is never a wise thing to do; it is certainly not a useful habit for a perfectionist!

I encourage trainee teachers to remember that the grades they are given following a lesson observation constitute only a few people's opinions, and although these views need to be valued and respected, they are subjective to what the observer constitutes as 'outstanding'. Therefore, it seems invaluable for teachers to be observed by a variety of people to collect different types of feedback.

There is an obvious positive element to this trait of aiming for faultlessness and of having high expectations of your pupils in the classroom (Teachers' Standard 1, DfE, 2013), but research, such as Stoeber & Rennert (2008), indicates that perfectionism in teachers is associated with high levels of stress and burnout, so let's explore perfectionism further.

There are two types of perfectionists, and they can be differentiated according to how they perceive or view mistakes: those that can cope with making mistakes, and those that can't. Only perfectionists who put pressure on themselves to not ever make mistakes and be perfect are likely to experience minimal personal accomplishment. This type of perfectionist may become cynical about their job and are at risk of physical and emotional difficulties. Their self-defeating thoughts take over when they make mistakes, and their thoughts of being a complete failure overpower them. That's the wrong kind of perfectionist!

Perfectionists who are not overly concerned about mistakes and do not feel the overpowering need to be accepted by everyone should not worry that their perfectionistic strivings will be detrimental to their wellbeing. Instead their perfectionism may, in fact, help them to actively cope with the challenges of their jobs. An example of this type of perfectionist would be that, although they strive for perfectionism, they are also able to look at a lesson observation that didn't go well as an opportunity for self-improvement. Some personality types perceive uncomfortable situations not as threats or stressors but as opportunities for personal growth and development.

> One of my past colleagues told me about mistakenly spelling a word incorrectly on the board whilst she had the audience of her class's parents during an open-day teaching session. Making this mistake was like water off a duck's back to her. However, I remember shuddering as she recounted the story to me, and I put myself in her position and imagined how I would have behaved and felt.
>
> I listened in wonderment as she described the moment that one of the parents, with a smirk on their face, raised their hand and commented, "Miss, you've spelt 'definitely' wrong." She had spelt it 'definately.'
>
> Apparently, my colleague laughed light-heartedly and replied, "Thanks for telling me... Wow, just another reminder of my humanity. I've made a mistake. It's no big deal. Now I know how to spell the word correctly!"
>
> This is a perfect example (but I thought you said 'perfect' doesn't exist!) of how to deal with making a mistake with humility and grace.

As previously mentioned, the first step to combating your perfectionist tendencies is to reflect upon whether you have any. If you're not sure, perhaps you could take one of the many quick tests online (for an example, see Useful resources).

In order to understand perfectionism more thoroughly, it helps to understand the characteristics, or traits, of perfectionism, followed by the consequences of being a perfectionist teacher. Next, you need to challenge your perfectionist thoughts and replace them with more realistic ones. Do you recognise any of the following common perfectionist traits? I'll use the context of lesson planning here:

1) Procrastination (You delay planning your lesson due to a fear of failure).
2) Excessive time spent on work (Your planning takes you an overly long time to complete).
3) Fault-finding (You focus upon anything that's not perfect about your lesson planning).

4) Goal-driven, not process-driven (You don't enjoy creating your lesson plans; you just see them as a means to an end).
5) Self-esteem based on performance, not inner worth (You feel you will only be a worthwhile teacher if you perform the lessons you have planned perfectly; the effort you've exerted or your good intentions are immaterial if the lesson doesn't go perfectly).

Try to remember that the negative type of perfectionism doesn't encourage growth, it restricts you and is damaging to your wellbeing; it depletes energy while it adds little value.

A potential consequence of perfectionism is burnout, as you can't keep up with your self-imposed excessively high standards. Other consequences could be lowered self-esteem, depression, anxiety and loss of life goals and/or pleasure in life, and perhaps increased feelings of isolation. It is likely that a constant drive for perfection will make you feel inadequate.

Children, and some parents, tend to think that teachers should be overflowing founts of knowledge. However, in my mind, this is not helpful. I feel that there is no shame in a teacher admitting that they do not understand something as comprehensively as they would like to. Afterall, encouraging a growth mindset (Dweck, 2008) is an idea that's widespread in schools, and, in our teacher-mode, we remind children daily that it is okay to not understand a concept or fact **yet.** Nevertheless, we often berate ourselves for not being perfect in every moment. Explaining to a child that you will need to research and find out the answer to something models a healthy and honest approach to learning. Indeed, learning should be viewed as a continual, lifelong process. Discovery and curiosity are the most exciting elements of learning rather than possessing the correct knowledge. The best Teachers' Standard (in my opinion) is 4B where as a teacher you 'promote a love of learning and children's intellectual curiosity.' (DfE, 2013). You should aim to have fun while you are teaching, as well as helping the children to gain a positive and enjoyable learning experience. Hold onto this, as it should keep you going if lessons do not go as perfectly as you had hoped.

To dismantle and squelch perfectionism, you need to notice and monitor your thoughts and dispute the perfectionistic ones. William James (1842–1910) wrote that 'the greatest weapon against stress is our ability to choose one thought over another', suggesting that there is a benefit to challenging our negative thought patterns. I recommend a useful sheet that displays a list of unhelpful thoughts and a replacement for each type (see Useful resources).

Step 8: No one is perfect!

In summary, it may be helpful to develop the habit of finding beauty in imperfection. Perfectionism is the misguided belief that if you attain perfection, then this will lead to happiness, and remember what I've told you about happiness? It's elusive.

Self-care

The reason I have included a section on 'self-care' is because I feel it is a neglected practice by many teachers who focus fully on the pupils in their class to the detriment of their own wellbeing. Putting children first then becomes a way of life and a habitual practice for teachers (Hazel, as cited in Carr, 2017). If this sounds familiar to you, perhaps you feel stuck in the pattern of neglecting yourself and powerless to change because you would not be performing effectively or according to the expectations of others. Boogren (2018:5) an American coach and educational speaker, has written a 'Self-care Action Plan for Educators' and states:

> …along your teaching (and life) journeys, you might have chosen students over yourself so many times that you've forgotten what it means to engage in consistent self-care without guilt.

Boogren (2018:3) emphasises that self-care practices need to be generally accepted by all educators, and the public, to:

> help ease the burden, lighten the load, honor the work, and sing the praises of hardworking, dedicated and passionate educators.
>
> (2018:3).

Self-care is your way to tend to and befriend yourself in the best way possible. It is not as basic as self-indulgence or pampering; there is a depth to self-care where you are consciously choosing behaviours that support and balance the effects of any emotional or physical stress in your life. Try thinking about self-care as 'protective factors' in your life that allow you to stay well. Self-care should be proactive and not in reaction to and in response to chronic stress and burnout. Although I have provided basic information in this book related to diet, exercise and rest, self-care is much more than making sure you get adequate rest and eat a nourishing diet. I would like the main amendment that you make to your life from reading this book to be developing compassion and care for yourself. I mean this in the way that you talk to yourself, how you learn to possess a noncritical, compassionate inner voice and in how you recognise and defend the changing needs that you have.

Sammons (2019) condones the need for schools to be more compassion-focused and explains that this would aid teacher wellbeing. He shares that we all have three main emotion-regulation systems that we move through in an attempt to manage our emotions: a threat system, a drive system and a soothing system. Sammons believes that teachers should learn to recognise when each system is being activated in them. He warns that if there is excessive pressure for teachers to fulfil punitive short-term goals based upon threats, alongside an underuse of the soothing system, then they will almost certainly be exposed to severe emotional stress. Sammons knows the consequences of this first-hand; the circumstances, in a school he taught in, drove him to suicidal thoughts and depression.

Due to teaching being so target-driven, schools can be a hard environment to thrive in with the threat of 'requires improvement' or 'inadequate'. Indeed, Ofsted's research (2019a) found that there were lower levels of wellbeing in teachers working in schools graded lower than 'good'. Everything is demanding you to be more motivated, to achieve the desired results and to ensure progression, and this can be overwhelming for both teachers and pupils. Sammons states that 'an over-reliance on the wrong measures has forced a serious misalignment of our core drivers as a profession' (2019a: 68). He thinks that human connections are the key to improvement; he explains that when a teacher loses connections to meaningful work, they become a passenger, and if they are in a toxic school environment, this can lead to isolation and unhealthy competition.

You can only know what works for you individually by exploring and experimenting with a variety of self-care strategies. However, it is crucial that self-care doesn't become another chore to add to a teacher's expanding list of jobs each day. For example, self-care activities should not be seen as similar to New Year's resolutions, which may add an element of guilt to your life if you don't succeed in keeping up with the intentions you have.

> *Self-care, to me, is merely about listening to my body so that I stop work with a 'good enough' attitude on days when I need to.*
>
> *I recently attended a stress-awareness workshop, which showed me how to develop in self-awareness. It urged me to know which times of the day I am the most creative and open to working hard, and which times I need to relax and give myself permission to slow down. The speaker explained that by attending to my needs when I am depleted would mean that I am operating at my optimum level at other times.*
>
> *Self-care ideas or offerings may come from other people, too. Once, a concerned and thoughtful friend of mine surprised me by leaving a little package outside my office. It contained:*
>
> - *A gift voucher for a specific book she thought I'd like,*
> - *A hot chocolate sachet,*
> - *Scented oil for a bath,*
> - *A craft kit,*
> - *And a letter about why she likes me.*

In summary, by having a handle on your own self-care, then you ensure that your needs are being met in case you haven't got people in your life or colleagues that will consider you. Self-care is a deliberate practice and takes discipline and effort but will allow you to have an autonomous approach to your wellbeing. As worthwhile changes emerge in your life, you will gain the personal knowledge about what recharges you. There is a strong possibility that with the addition of a dose of self-care, your productivity, competence and resilience as a teacher would improve.

Resilience

The National Resilience Institution define human resilience as:

> The capacity to prepare for, adapt to and grow through trauma, disruption or loss.

Emotional resilience can be developed and comprises of skills we can learn such as being reflective, self-aware, optimistic and having a sense of humour. Charney (2012) shared that there are 10 factors that create resilience. I have summarised the ones that I feel are most significant to the role of a teacher:

- a moral compass, ethics and altruism to know what is right for you
- optimism and belief in a brighter future
- an ability to leave your comfort zone and to possess an adaptive response to fear
- a sense of life meaning, purpose and growth
- a practice for overcoming challenges and gaining social support
- cognitive and emotional flexibility

Greenfield (2015) developed a model for teacher resilience and shared that resilience shouldn't be seen in an individual light, but as relational. This study found that the resilience of a teacher very much depends on the environment of the school; it relies on the support provided, both from colleagues, school leaders and within the broader context of the school, also comprising of policy and politics. In addition, it was found that teacher resilience involves the interactions between relationships, thoughts, challenges and actions.

Thankfully, in the ESP's 'Teacher Wellbeing Index' (2019:28), 64% of educational professionals described themselves as having high resilience levels. School leaders had the highest resilience levels at 72%.

Self-efficacy is vital for teacher resilience and varies according to how competent a teacher feels they are. The term 'self-efficacy' was coined by Bandura (1995) and can be seen as your own beliefs in your capacity to influence change in your life. The significant people in our lives can either weaken or strengthen our self-efficacy according to how we think people see us. Therefore, it is important to imagine, and believe, that we can succeed, even through the eyes of others.

Step 9: Your lifestyle choices

I've highlighted the importance of developing a personal approach to self-care, and there's no difference when it comes to eating and sleeping. Therefore, it's worth working out what food makes you feel good and what the best evening routine is for you so that sleep arrives easily. If you're interested in maintaining optimal health and wellbeing, then you need to make from seven to nine hours of sleep a night a top priority in your life. Please take these ideas with a pinch of salt though (although only a pinch, because too much salt is bad for your health!). Please drop the following suggestions if they don't resonate with your own ideas of wellbeing. If you are working in a toxic environment where stress is prevalent within your school, no amount of sleep or positive lifestyle choices will counteract this, but still it is worth being aware of how you look after yourself to maintain as healthy a body as you can.

Sleep

You need adequate sleep to be able to face the day, feel refreshed and have enough energy at school. Without sufficient sleep, you will be below par in terms of your lesson delivery and your patience will be frayed (and it's important to have plenty of patience as a teacher!). Insomnia is often the first indication that your mental health has slipped, so keep a watch for any disruption of your sleeping patterns. Fifty-two percent of educational professionals experience insomnia or difficulty sleeping in the ESP's 'Teacher Wellbeing Index' (2019:32), which had risen from 28% the previous year, suggesting that a focus on sleep is warranted.

There is much you can do to encourage deep, undisturbed sleep, and hopefully there will be some strategies from the below section that you can take (and add to Step 6) to promote your wellbeing.

Tips to encourage a good night's sleep—think 'STRIPES' (you know how I love an acronym by now!)

Self-care

The forms of self-care I've already mentioned may contribute to your ability to unwind for the day and allow you to transition into a relaxed state, ready for sleep. For example, you might listen to music, read a book or take a warm aromatherapy bath with Epsom salts dissolved in it. The salts detox and calm the body. Remember to do all the jobs you need to do before bed though (for example, brush your teeth before the bath), as you can feel really drowsy after a salty soak!

Technology out

Reduce your blue-light exposure in the evenings, as it tricks your body into thinking it is still daytime. Either avoid using electronic devices or watching television for at least two hours before bed, or get an app on your laptop or phone that removes blue and green light (see Useful resources). You can also buy glasses that block the blue light from devices.

Routine

Try to maintain a consistent time that you sleep and wake in the morning so that your body cycle remains in sync. Although short naps in the day are good for your brain, try not to take naps that are longer than 30 minutes as this can negatively impact the quality of your nighttime sleep and confuse your internal body clock.

Insomnia advice

If you struggle with insomnia, then visit your GP so that they can rule out an underlying health condition causing it. Your GP may offer you sleep aids such as melatonin (a hormone that helps promote sleep) or a magnesium supplement.

Position

I'm talking about the position you sleep in here—and nothing else! Seriously though, how you sleep has an impact on your health. For instance, the best way to sleep is on your back, as it prevents back and neck pain and reduces the chance of acid reflux. Sleeping on your side is fine, but you'll need a thick pillow to support your neck adequately. Sleeping on your stomach is less desirable for your health as it puts stress on your spine, muscles and joints. It's best to have a very thin pillow if you sleep like this. It may be worth investing in a good quality mattress that supports your body in the way you desire.

> I recall my dad saying that if you were to spend your money on only two things in life, it should be on an expensive, high-quality mattress and costly, comfortable shoes because if you're not in one, then you're in the other. What about slippers, dad?

You might have a fight on your hands, though, if you have a partner and they prefer a softer mattress than you or vice versa. However, I do believe you can purchase double mattresses that are different on each side. In Sweden, many couples have separate duvets in a double bed so that if one spouse fidgets and moves the covers then this doesn't disturb the other person in the bed.

Environment

Ideally, your room should be cool (between 18 and 24 degrees Celsius), clutter-free, dark and quiet. Consider fitting blackout blinds in the bedroom or wearing an eye mask or earplugs. If you like the smell of lavender, add a few drops of lavender oil to your pillow. Email notifications should not disturb the quiet atmosphere you create and will only draw your attention back to thoughts of work and busyness. A bedroom should be dedicated only to sleep and intimacy so that you'll foster a peaceful environment conducive to rest and pleasure. I discuss the benefits of meditation and mindfulness later in this book, which can be an effective way to slow down the body and mind prior to your slumber. Progressive relaxation techniques work well too, but move from your head downwards to relax, as moving from your toes upwards can energise you instead. I also discuss the benefits of exercise later in this book, one of which is that it improves your sleep, but it should not be undertaken too close to your bedtime.

Snacks

Don't drink caffeinated drinks after 3pm, as levels of caffeine can stay elevated in your bloodstream for up to eight hours. Caffeine stimulates your nervous system and therefore will not help. If you crave the taste of coffee, try decaffeinated varieties instead. Alcohol tends to negatively affect your sleep too, so it is worth limiting it. It may not be to everyone's taste, but a chamomile tea is widely regarded as a mild tranquilizer, as the sedative effects of flavonoid and apigenin bind to benzodiazepine receptors in the brain. Clever stuff!

Reducing your fluid intake a few hours before you hit the sack could help too, as it will avoid nocturia (which is the fancy name for excessive urination during the night). Eating a meal close to bedtime can affect the quality of your sleep. However, the snack that you eat before bed may help you to relax. The next section outlines a few considerations for you to make regarding your overall diet, but as an introduction, the following foods are beneficial to promote sleep:

- A banana (high in potassium, which helps to keep you asleep and tryptophan and magnesium, which are natural sedatives).
- Fruit with low-fat yogurt and Brazil nuts, which contain selenium to protect you from the damage caused by oxidative stress. (You only need two Brazil nuts to gain the optimum daily dose of selenium.)
- A whole-grain sandwich with turkey and lettuce. Turkey contains tryptophan, which is an amino acid that helps your body make serotonin (a relaxing mood hormone), which then helps your body make melatonin (a hormone that controls sleep cycles). What a good excuse to eat lots of it at Christmas! Lettuce contains a substance called lactur carium that helps promote sleep by sedating the nervous system.
- A bowl of cherries, as they are one of only a few foods that contain melatonin, so they make a perfect snack before bed (if you can afford them, and if they are in season!).

Food

Let's start by discussing what constitutes an ideal diet, although I am conscious that we are often given mixed messages about nutrition and what a perfect meal looks like. I intend to delve into the fundamentals related to the science of food with a focus only on its relationship to our mood. Diet has a massive connection with the hippocampus, a part of the brain that is key to our mental health. I won't cover the complexities related to the links between food and our physical health, particularly because I am not qualified in this. I wish only to introduce the idea to you that when addressing our wellbeing, it is worth paying attention to what we put into our bodies and to develop an awareness about how certain foods make us feel. I apologise if I have oversimplified any aspects.

Gillian McKeith famously said, 'you are what you eat', but I would revise this to 'you are the nutrients you absorb'. Everyone's body is different and reacts to food in unique ways.

Western eating habits have often been criticised. In basic terms, a healthy diet constitutes of plenty of fresh fruit and vegetables, low saturated fat and salt, plenty of water and foods rich in vitamins and nutrients. It is also worth keeping your BMI (Body Mass Index) in the healthy zone.

Overall, a Mediterranean diet seems to come out on top. The Global Burden of Disease (2019) published a report on the diet of people aged 25 or over across 195 countries from 1990 to 2017. They found that we don't eat enough whole grains, fruit, vegetables, legumes, nuts and seeds, and we overconsume processed meat, sugar-sweetened beverages and salt.

Let's begin by reflecting upon what needs thought when it comes to designing meal choices to suit us and our mental health needs. Here's a bit of science:

- *Macronutrients*: In the most basic of terms, we need macronutrients to gain energy for our bodies to work well. The macronutrients that are important for energy are carbohydrates, protein and fats. Fibre is not considered as crucial for energy but is essential, especially for the health of our gut.
- *Micronutrients*: Vitamins and minerals are micronutrients and are mostly consumed in dairy products, plant oils, fruits and vegetables. These are significant for our mental health; for example, Vitamin D is a fat-soluble hormone that has been found to reduce depression because it regulates mood. The effects of Vitamin D have been linked to Seasonal Affective Disorder (SAD), which is a mood disorder featuring depressive symptoms. SAD has been found to coincide with sudden drops of Vitamin D in the body during times of the year when there is relatively little sunshine. These changing levels of Vitamin D3 are thought to affect serotonin levels in the brain. It can help us to remember the positive effects of a walk in the fresh air and sunlight during winter months.

  A mineral that has been found to regulate blood pressure is magnesium, and it can help with relaxation and insomnia, as already mentioned. You can find magnesium in whole wheat, dark chocolate, spinach, quinoa, almonds, cashews and peanuts, amongst other things.
- *Phytochemicals*: These are naturally occurring bioactive compounds. They can be found in fruit, vegetables, grains, legumes, nuts, seeds and other plant foods and have many potential benefits for our mental and brain health.

Our diet can be influenced by many things: our biology, environment, personal values and beliefs, social setting and how much money we have, therefore we need to find one that suits us personally. However, we do need to be critical when it comes to assessing diets, as some of them over the years have been extremely restrictive and not with a focus on health at all. For example, the Cigarette Diet from the 1920s encouraged women to reach for a cigarette instead of something sweet to manage their weight!

- *Anti-inflammatory foods:* This book will only explore one example of an approach to eating, that I have found very beneficial to my health, and that is to eat as many anti-inflammatory foods as is possible; in other words, avoid or limit foods that cause inflammation in the body. It is a simple way to eat and requires minimal effort, so it will suit a busy teacher who hasn't time to slave away in the kitchen. There's no calorie counting or food weighing, and its focus is on healthy eating to sustain a healthy body rather than on weight loss. It has been suggested that 7 out of 10 adults have never heard of this diet despite it having been recommended by health care professionals for years.

The basic principles of this diet choice are as follows:

- Inflammation is how the body responds to something harmful such as injury, infection or exposure to harmful substances that your body finds a threat.
- Our immune system is designed to support us when we need repairing, and any inflammation in our bodies increases the risk of disease and even depression and anxiety, especially if it is chronic and long-term.
- Inflammation is a chronic activation of the body's immune system. It is clear that prolonged stress could lead to a chronic inflammatory state and, therefore, eating anti-inflammatory foods could significantly contribute to decreasing the state of inflammation in the body.
- The gut is the engine of our immune systems, and so, when we are stressed, it effects our gut and vice versa. The food group that has shown a promising effect on gut health is fermented foods, such as yoghurt, kefir, tempeh, kimchi, miso and kvass. Probiotics (friendly bacteria) or

prebiotics are also essential for gut health. The best sources of prebiotics include artichokes, beans, leeks, onions, bananas and whole wheat.
- A Mediterranean diet is consistently associated with a decrease in pro-inflammatory response. This suggests that these diets—high in plant-based food and fish—may decrease the risks of mental or emotional disorders. In fact, the SMILES trial (2017) provided evidence that diet quality (a Mediterranean diet) was directly associated with mental health across different cultures and life stages. Studies such as this one have shown that a higher intake of fruit, vegetables, whole grains and fish and lower intakes of highly processed and sugary foods were consistently associated with better mental health outcomes. Fish and seafood are essential sources of Omega-3 fatty acids and phytochemicals, which are also important characteristics of an anti-inflammatory diet.

Here are a few essential instructions if you wish to follow an anti-inflammatory diet:

- Eat healthy unsaturated fats, such as monounsaturated fats (found in olive oil and avocado etc) or polyunsaturated fats, such as Omega-3 (found in salmon etc). In fact, olive oil has been shown to fight inflammation even better than ibuprofen due to the compound in it called oleocanthal! Omega-6 is also a polyunsaturated fat, but ideally one should choose foods high in Omega-3 but low in Omega-6 (like salmon and tuna). Some foods, like catfish, sunflower oil, margarine and ready-meals, are high in Omega-6, so are best avoided.
- Eat a whole-food diet (fruits and vegetables) with limited processed foods.
- Keep to the following proportions: 30% of your calorie intake should be from healthy fats, 20-30% from protein and 40-50% from carbohydrates.

It helps me to look at my hand when deciding how much to eat. You might think this is strange, but it helps to get each meal in proportion:

Your palm determines your protein portions.

Your fist determines your vegetable portion.

Your cupped hand determines your carbohydrate portions.

Your thumb determines your fat portions.

If you are male, then you double these values, for example, two of your palms determines your protein portions etc.

- Eat the best types of carbs such as complex carbs like brown rice, beans, broccoli, sweet potato etc and limit simple carbs, which have had the fibre stripped from them, such as white rice, white pasta and white bread.
- Eat lean protein such as chicken, turkey and Greek yoghurt, which strengthens the body's defences against infection and disease.
- Eat plenty of fibre, as it has been found to reverse years of damage from chronic inflammation. Aim for 40 grams of daily fibre in foods such as whole grains, berries and beans.
- Consume minimal sugar, which massively increases inflammation in your body (you'd probably guessed that!). If you have a sweet tooth, then opt for natural sweeteners such as agave nectar or molasses. Dark chocolate (over 70% cocoa content) is your best choice as it contains phytochemicals from the cocoa plant.
- Choose red wine (especially Pinot Noir) over other alcoholic drinks, as it contains phytonutrients, as does white or green tea (making it a healthier choice rather than coffee) and soy-based products.
- Drink plenty of water, particularly spring water, as it drives the inflammation out of the cells in our bodies and is essential for the proper circulation of nutrients in the body. If you're like me and find it rather laborious to drink enough water, then try adding a few slices of lemon or lime or a sprig of mint for flavour.

Examples of meals

I have provided a few ideas of the types of breakfast, lunch, main meal and snack to sustain health. Apologies if you are vegan, vegetarian or pescatarian, as some of these ideas will require adaption. I have outlined the nutritional properties/benefits related to the ingredients to get you thinking about how to combine different healthy food items. I have veered towards including anti-inflammatory foods, but my focus is primarily on encouraging positive mental health. However, if you wish to learn more about specific anti-inflammatory meal choices, then there are many good books on the market that share ideas for simple recipes to enjoy.

To wake you up in the morning

My TA referred to me as 'Lemon Lady' as every morning, I would walk into the classroom with my flask of hot water and lemon.

I swear by a drink of hot water and freshly squeezed lemon in the morning. It cleanses your internal organs—especially your digestive system—freshens your breath and generally perks you up. You want some science, do you? Here it goes... The biggest lemon-water benefit may be from the temperature of the water and not even the added lemon. Drinking any water, especially warm water, first thing in the morning can help flush the digestive system and rehydrate the body. As a rich source of Vitamin C, lemon juice protects the body from immune-system deficiencies. Other benefits include its powerful antibacterial properties (to fight infections), its ability to cleanse the liver (to flush out toxins) and its help in regulating natural bowel movement (to... well, you know).

In addition, part of an effective morning routine (and this is nothing to do with food, and portrays me as cruel) can be to turn the shower onto freezing cold for a few seconds; it can work wonders. The cold water makes your hair shine and wakes up your body. It improves your circulation, boosts weight loss and fires up your immune system.

Breakfast ideas

Eggs are a wonderful source of protein to give you energy to fuel your day. Try Eggsperimenting with omelettes (☺) by adding vegetables such as tomatoes, peppers and mushrooms. I add shiitake mushrooms to as many of my meals as I can, as they contain potent anti-cancer properties. They tend to be a little chewy and slimy, but I've grown accustomed to them. Eggs and smashed avocado on whole-meal toast makes for a good breakfast. Smoothies and porridge oats with chia seeds are a good option too. Blueberries are extremely anti-inflammatory and can be added to muesli or granola with a dollop of yoghurt.

Lunch ideas

Obviously, salads are a good choice for lunch, especially if you combine these with essential proteins like chicken, mackerel, tuna or feta cheese.

Spinach and watercress are loaded with anti-inflammatory compounds. Try hummus dip with carrots, celery and broccoli and whole-wheat toasted pita. The combination of chickpeas, sesame seed paste, oil and lemon makes hummus a good source of energy, complex carbs, healthy fats and fibre.

Main meals

Meals that are high in protein are ideal, such as salmon and vegetables. Choose sweet potatoes rather than white potatoes; sweet potatoes have a variety of beneficial components such as high amounts of antioxidants, beta-carotene and fibre. Turkey is calming, and here are a few ideas for meals with it:

- Turkey chilli with brown rice is a great slow-cooker choice so that the smell greets you the moment you walk in from school.
- Stuffed peppers with turkey mince, quinoa, mozzarella, spinach, Italian seasoning and garlic.

Snacks

Dark chocolate and popcorn make a good snack if you are craving something sweet. The antioxidants in cocoa increases blood flow and can help reduce mental fatigue and improve mood. Popcorn is high in fibre. Similarly, a handful of nuts are a good choice for a snack.

Exercise

I felt that it was necessary to include a short section on exercise in this book because staying active can massively impact on a teacher's wellbeing in terms of physical health, but also as a mood booster. Physical activity has been found to be helpful in stimulating the production of chemicals in the brain called endorphins. These can help lift your mood, give you more energy and make you feel a sense of pleasure and satisfaction. Endorphins are released during exercise (and also during sex), when you feel fearful, when you laugh and when you eat chocolate.

In the ESP's 'Teacher Wellbeing Index' (2019:42) exercise was reported to be the most popular way of coping; it had been the most popular way to alleviate problems in the last three years in the 'Teacher Wellbeing Index' results. Exercise can act as an antidote to depression, anxiety, stress and post-traumatic stress disorder. In fact, outdoor exercise (or ecotherapy) has been found to be as effective as anti-depressants in treating mild to moderate depression. Montgomery et al. (2012) found that among student teachers, those that were engaging in aerobic exercise and strength training experienced lower stress levels around workload, thereby indicating that exercise is a useful coping strategy.

Wilson (2019) wrote about the powerful impact that exercise, particularly swimming for 20 minutes in the ocean and hiking regularly, had on her chronic anxiety. The secret to sticking to an exercise schedule is to find the right type of exercise for you; not all of us have the ocean at our disposal. If you keep active when you are doing household chores such as the cleaning, vacuuming and gardening, then you are ticking off jobs at the same time as getting your exercise quota. Perhaps you can exercise with a friend or partner so that you are mixing social time with exercise and find an exercise that injects fun into your life.

Read the account below written by a busy teacher about how exercise was her saviour:

> Sport and exercise have been part of my life for as long as I can remember. There have only been a handful of times when I haven't been able to continue my passions for hockey and running; whilst pregnant, injured and, sadly, at times when my working life seemed to take over. It's frustrating not to participate in sport due to workload, time and lack of energy stemming from work and general life!
>
> It is widely known that exercise releases endorphins into the body, and in turn, it can make you feel better, and for me, it was true. The times when I couldn't exercise led me into a spiral of difficulties with both my physical and mental health. There was a long period during my mid-thirties where I just couldn't find the time or energy to fit in any exercise, and when I look back now, I can see I let teaching take over my life. After a time of really struggling with depression and an eating disorder, I took perspective on my life, realising I wasn't well and that I had to do

something about it. I could also see the knock-on effect for my family; we all needed me to do something and luckily, I had the support of my husband to do it.

Firstly, I took back control and planned in times for exercise; I physically put exercise slots in my diary and stuck to them as much as I could. I left work slightly earlier and marked at home. I kept reminding myself that, after an exercise day, I was more efficient in the classroom. I began squeezing in 20-30 mins of exercise, whether this was at the gym or a quick run before I picked my kids up; in the summer months, I'd pick them up from their childcare/school and take them to the park and whilst they played, I would run laps and use the play equipment to exercise. In the wetter, darker months, I'd give the kids their tea and do an exercise DVD. Whilst some might say I wasted quality time with my children, I would argue that my children have seen me manage to work full-time and lead a healthy, active lifestyle; it actually became the norm for them and still is!

I used to beat myself up about missing my time to exercise, but now I know it doesn't matter, I'm not going to balloon four dress sizes or be unable to get up the stairs anymore. Instead, as soon as possible, I get back on it. As the children have got older, it is a little easier to fit some exercise in; it's just a case of grabbing the moment and maximising the time I have. More recently, a work friend and I have made a concerted effort to go for a run after work, even when we are both tired, have had bad days and really just want to go home and curl up. One of us (usually me!) gets us out so we run off the day's worries and go home to our families in a better state of mind. My social life is my sport and exercise; I don't go 'out' often, so this is another reason I am adamant to continue fitting it into my life.

Playing hockey is a little trickier than running because I am governed by the training night of the club and playing matches on a Saturday. I am Ladies Captain at my hockey club and have been for a number of years. With my husband working away quite a lot, I often have to take the kids with me to training. They seem to love being there; when they were younger, they would play on scooters at the side of the pitch whilst I trained. Luckily my coach and teammates are really understanding, and my kids are our main supporters! They literally have grown up on the side of the hockey pitch and it hasn't done them any harm (not that I have noticed yet!).

> I am proof that full-time working women, especially teachers, can continue to compete in sport. The benefits are massive for me, especially during those dark few years through the depression and eating disorder. The 'team' aspect of hockey helps my mental health as well as the obvious physical fitness that comes with hockey. Sometimes on a Saturday, trying to get myself ready to leave early in the morning, ensuring the kids have everything they need, can be exhausting, and at times it can all feel too much, but once I am with the team and on that pitch, it is soon forgotten. I go home after a match feeling a better person, a better mother and better wife, although if we lose the match, this can be slightly different!
>
> Teaching is a rewarding but exhausting job. As teachers, we are role models to those we teach, so let's be role models with our work-life balance. I strongly encourage everyone to do something active a couple of times a week; you will reap the benefits and so will your employer and your family.

Finally, in order to sustain an exercise routine, it is useful to remember how amazing you feel during and after the exercise so that the memory of that feeling encourages you to continue to exercise regularly. The most difficult part of incorporating exercise into a busy life is overcoming a variety of obstacles, such as…

- Feeling too <u>exhausted</u>: Exercise doesn't make sense when you are bone-tired, but the truth is that physical activity is a powerful energiser. Try to schedule the exercise at the time in the day when you have the most energy, though.
- Feeling <u>overwhelmed</u>: If exercise just feels like another obligation, then it pays to remember that exercise actually helps our productivity.
- Feeling <u>out-of-shape</u>: starting with low-impact movement is a good idea, and this will build your confidence. Even a short walk has benefits for your wellbeing.
- Feeling <u>pain</u>: If you are experiencing pain or mobility problems, then consult with a professional about the most suitable way for you to exercise safely, like in the water, so your body is supported.

People who exercise often report that exercise allows them to escape or interrupt the flow of worries in their mind. Walking can provide the space to tame the clutter of negative thoughts that may have accumulated. Exercise can be paired with mindfulness in different ways, such as noticing the rhythm of your breathing, the repetitive sounds of your feet, or the sensation of the wind on your face. Meditation and mindfulness scored as the second most popular way that educational professionals dealt with negative symptoms experienced at work (ESP's 'Teacher Wellbeing Index' [2019:42]). This, therefore, justifies more explanation on the value of mindfulness and the practical application of it.

Mindfulness

Mental health is about the human condition, and the more you learn about the brain, the more you can accept, understand and own the way you feel. Much research has been shared about the positive effects of mindfulness on the brain (Wax, 2016). It has been found that mindfulness practice changes the brain; indeed, the brain changes according to every experience and thought we have. When teaching, our minds may be in a constant state of flux, but we can self-regulate and add attentional focus using mindfulness. Becoming mindful will help us to gain space so we thoughtfully respond to situations in our busy days, rather than reacting habitually.

Mindfulness is about present-moment awareness. It is about noticing your thoughts and bringing your consciousness back to the now. Meditation is a more formal process and may involve sitting (in a relaxed but alert posture) and bringing your focus back time and again to, for example, your breath, a taste, a sound, a smell. It is useful to choose the breath to anchor us as it is always there. Mindfulness is more informal and can be incorporated into a busy day where you stop and let go of future worries and past regrets.

Thich Nhat Hanh & Weare (2017: xi) write in their book, *Happy teachers change the world: A guide for cultivating mindfulness in education*, that:

> teachers who study mindfulness tend to experience fewer mental health problems...report greater wellbeing, including a sense of calmness, life satisfaction, self-confidence and self-compassion...greater empathy,

tolerance, forgiveness and less anger and hostility. Their cognitive performance improves, including their ability to pay attention and focus, make decisions, and respond flexibly to challenges.

Weare continues to list other benefits, such as being 'more attuned' to students' needs and having better physical health. Each time you are mindful, you are exercising the brain; you are developing in self-awareness and learning to control it rather than letting it control you.

It is clear that mindfulness on paper sounds like a useful thing to practice, but it may not be something that you feel would come naturally to you.

> Once, I forced my husband to sit quietly, close his eyes and concentrate on his breathing. He dissolved into a fit of giggles after about half a minute, so I relented and accepted that it probably was not his idea of relaxation. Similarly, when I trained in massage therapy and I asked if I could practice an aromatherapy massage on him, his response was 'okay, as long as it's quick'; whereas I know many people would have relished the opportunity of a free massage, he has admitted to not really feeling any benefit from massage or, in his words, being 'mauled'. His personal idea of relaxation is listening to music or playing his guitar. Nevertheless, I believe that when he plays the guitar, he is being mindful; he insists that he has to be fully in the moment (or 'in the zone') to play well and maintain the focus that is necessary.
>
> I try to meditate as much as I can before the mayhem of my day. I also try to have short sleeps or 'nano-naps' in the afternoon during the weekends, which tend to recharge my mind and relax my body. I also find that walking my dog at night is a kind of mindfulness activity for me. It involves both me 'numbing-out' and trying to locate some space and emptiness in my mind, but it also involves me trying to 'feel' in terms of what is happening in my body and mind. My dog-walk every evening is my 'check-in' where I experience some solitary time (with just canine company) to process the day's events and to 'let go' of any thoughts that are unhelpful. I also find that I seem to sleep better after this quick burst of exercise and fresh air and, as I very rarely engage in any cardiovascular exercise, I try to run as fast as I can on the last stretch of the walk, when I can see my house ahead of me for motivation.

Three examples of practical mindfulness activities

Repetition

Select two tasks that you engage in on a daily basis, for example, cleaning the kitchen sideboard, washing-up, brushing your teeth or eating a piece of fruit. Attempt to remember and remain mindful whilst doing them. Check in with your body and mind (you'll be getting good at this, especially if you have been using the 'check-in' questions you formulated in Step 1). Notice anything that is happening in your internal and external worlds. Try to 'let go' of anything unnecessary, take a few deep breaths and focus your attention on the task at hand. For instance, if you are washing-up, think about how the warm, foamy water feels on your hands and the sensations it evokes. Perhaps it smells lemony or feels soft on your skin. When your attention wanders, gently acknowledge this distraction and bring your attention back to the moment.

Retreat

Set aside 10 minutes and escape to a quiet place in your house or classroom. Light a candle (maybe a battery-operated one if you are in school). Close your eyes, or leave them open if you are self-conscious. Make sure your feet are planted on the floor, your back is straight, and your hands are laid gently in your lap. Spend five minutes in a mindful state using your breath as an anchor point. As you breathe in, silently think 'in', and as you breathe out, think 'out'. Notice the pauses in between the inhaling and exhaling. Feel the cool air as it enters your nostrils, and notice the warm air as you exhale. During the remaining five minutes, imagine that a golden light is shining down on you from above and is warming your body and melting away any tension in your body or mind. Imagining a safe place in your mind may help you to feel a sense of peace.

> I love acer plants (also called Japanese maples), so I picture a lake with the sun shining on the water and gleaming on the leaves of a red acer plant.

You may have somewhere more exotic to imagine. Try to evoke the smells, sights, sounds and touch of the place you have retreated to. Enjoy the feeling for a while and then open your eyes, stand up slowly and stretch. Get yourself a nice, cold glass of water (hopefully you have a water cooler at school) and go about the rest of your day. I guarantee you will feel much better than you had 10 minutes before!

One school I read about has meditation pods situated around the school grounds, for both teachers and children to use. Ocean sounds and relaxing music can be played inside them. They offer a quiet, safe place to retreat to be alone and rest.

Watching the sky—the pleasure of big things!

If meditation and mindfulness is not suited to you, then just finding pleasure and joy in simple everyday pursuits may inject some positivity into your life, especially if currently your life feels consumed by everything 'teaching'. Start with finding small things that excite you, for instance, enjoying a morning cuppa sitting in the sun, watching the birds in your garden splash in the birdbath and watching the clouds move across the sky. Your mind will start to settle the more you practice noticing these things that bring you pleasure, and your wellbeing will improve. Recall that your philosophy is to work in order to live, rather than to live for work. I doubt you will ever be on your deathbed wishing you had worked more, so remember to have fun, keep perspective and don't take your life for granted.

> My Buddhist teacher reminded me to wake in the morning and rather than thinking 'I won't die today' to think 'I may die today,' and use that fact to inform my daily decisions. You might think that this sounds a bit morbid, but nevertheless, it gave me perspective.
>
> Unfortunately, most of us need to work to sustain our lives and to finance everything in it. However, if doesn't hurt to remember that work is merely a means to an end. We are lucky if we choose something that we enjoy for our work, but it is up to us to enjoy it as much as we can. It was on days when I felt overwhelmed and frustrated with teaching that I found spending 10 minutes looking at the sky extremely useful. Sometimes I gazed out of my classroom window marvelling at the space,

> beauty and magnitude to give me added perspective. Sometimes I'd lie on my back in my garden after a school day and observe the sky and watch the clouds, the flight of birds or observe the raindrops falling onto my face. This seemed to allow me to gain perspective of my worries and maintain a mindful awareness in times of stress; after all, the sky is always available to me. The great expanse of the sky makes me feel small and insignificant, but also makes the majority of my worries feel insignificant and fleeting. I reflect on the sky being ever-changing, like my mind, and how different it looks according to the weather. Burch & Penman (2013:100) enjoy this practice too and comment that, 'It does not matter whether the sky is clear and sunny or grey and overcast. It is always full of shifting patterns, even if they are not apparent at first.'

Classroom calm

I feel optimistic about the recent government changes about teaching mental health and wellbeing in primary schools. Aspects of Personal, Social, Health and Economic Education (PSHE) have been made compulsory. The guidance provided in the PSHE Association paper (funded by the DfE) called *Teacher guidance: teaching about mental health and emotional wellbeing* (2019a) (in Useful resources) will be valuable for you to refer to. The document was designed to increase the confidence of teachers in the delivery of wellbeing lessons (you can access some useful lesson plans to adapt for your class), as it was recognised that teachers may find it 'challenging' (2019a:5) to teach about mental health. I can particularly recommend the services and free school resources offered by the Charlie Waller Memorial Trust (see Useful resources).

Making the classroom environment as pleasant as possible may increase wellbeing. Consider adding plants to corners of the room, as they release oxygen into the air and add a natural touch to the surroundings. A 'calming' quiet area of your classroom is useful when de-escalating behavioural issues or allowing children time to self-regulate emotions. This area may contain for instance, a beanbag, aromatherapy playdough and headphones for playing relaxing music.

If you are dealing with challenging behaviour on a regular basis, make sure that you are utilising all the support from colleagues that you can. For your own wellbeing, it is important that you never respond emotionally to challenging behaviour and you keep a dignified and controlled demeanour. Always remember to separate the child from their behavior, and don't take their actions personally. Use positive language and explicit positive praise. Provide simple direction for children that is respectful but firm and display the congruent body language. Your behaviour management approach should be consistent and decisive, which will allow children to feel safe. Giving children choices (not threats) and opportunities to own their behaviour is helpful and encourages autonomy. Include chances for pupils, during the day, to discuss their emotional climate and feelings; you may encourage them to do a 'check-in' on how they are feeling, within their body and mind, throughout the day.

Useful resources

- I recommend the reading of this report (2019) (which is only 16 pages long) from Anna Freud National Centre for Children and Families and can be downloaded at https://www.annafreud.org/media/7653/3rdanna-freud-booklet-staff-wellbeing-web-pdf-21-june.pdf
- Charlie Waller Memorial Trust, found at: https://www.cwmt.org.uk/school-training. They will send printed leaflets and resources to your school for free and provide excellent speakers that will visit your school for a donation to the Trust.
- The following website has many ideas about incorporating wellbeing strategies into primary schools, and therefore is worth an online visit: https://www.mentallyhealthyschools.org.uk/
- Flux or f.lux (https://justgetflux.com/) removes blue and green light.
- The quiz to find out if you're a perfectionist is based upon 10 simple questions and is aptly called *Are you a Perfectionist?* You can find it at- https://www.verywellmind.com/quiz-are-you-a-perfectionist-4006910?quizResult=cc84dbcc
- This sheet has often helped me to address the frequent types of unhelpful thoughts I have in my mind and shows me how to challenge them. It can be found at: https://www.getselfhelp.co.uk/docs/UnhelpfulThinkingHabitsWithAlternatives.pdf
- For mindfulness books, I endorse any book by Jon Kabat-Zinn who founded the practice Mindfulness Based Stress reduction in 1979,

where he combined Buddhist teachings and science, to create a very well-received practice that helped countless people handle physical and emotional pain. Pema Chodrin is one of my favourite authors; she is a Buddhist nun and writes using a very down-to-earth style using very expressive language, including some expletives!

- Mental Health Foundation, How to… guides, are short evidence-based guides on sleep, exercise, mindfulness, exercise, stress management, later life and anxiety, found at: www.mentalhealth.org.uk/howto They are £1.50 each as online booklets.
- Pugh, V. et al (2020), *My life: Key Stage 1 Primary PSHE Handbook*, Collins, This is an example of the KS1 scheme and details of pricing for schools can be found at: https://www.amazon.co.uk/My-Life-Stage-Primary-Handbook/dp/0008378886/ref=sr_1_12?keywords=victoria+pugh&qid=1585090585&sr=8-12

Takeaway message: Should a teacher role-model wellbeing?

Remembering the following has helped me in recent months when I have felt overburdened, and it has reaffirmed my resolution to ensure my own wellbeing takes precedence…

All teachers are in the unique position of influencing the future happiness and success of the next generation. As a teacher, you act as a role model, not just in the academic sense but also in how you manage your own emotions and cope with stress. Teachers can impart strategies to teach pupil resilience, self-efficacy and incorporate wellbeing into their classroom practice to allow children to learn how to deal with the unpredictable challenges of life. Therefore, it is crucial that you don't overlook your own wellbeing or else you may fail your pupils. School leaders are the next focus in this book, both in terms of how they support staff but also in how they look after themselves and role model wellbeing to their staff…

PART 3

A PERSONAL PLAN FOR WELLBEING

5

HOW CAN YOU PLAN FOR SUSTAINED TEACHER WELLBEING?

School leaders supporting teacher wellbeing

If you are reading this as a school leader, grab a hot drink and a nice snack and digest the following content, knowing that it is meant in a wholly positive way. If the teacher wellbeing in your school is at an all-time low, don't be discouraged or direct blame at yourself; just take a deep breath and start from where your school currently is. The fact that you have decided to read this book (and reached Chapter 5) is a sign that positive wellbeing changes are ahead for your school.

On the flipside, if you already pride yourself at being successful in supporting the staff wellbeing at your school, then you should be proud and celebrate what you and your staff have achieved. Accomplishing teacher wellbeing in a school, especially in the recent educational climate, is something special and should be applauded. I hope that you have not achieved this at the detriment of your own wellbeing, though. I have met school leaders that give everything of themselves and work tirelessly for the good of a school and, in doing so, neglect their own wellbeing in the process.

There is a section at the end of this chapter about how the wellbeing of school leaders can be supported.

Arguably, the most important asset in each school is their staff, and therefore, the wellbeing of staff should be promoted and safeguarded. It is important for you to accept that everyone is at risk of low wellbeing. However, there is only so much a manager can do, especially if the main negative impact on the wellbeing of a staff member is of a personal nature. You are doing well if, within the boundaries of your role, you are:

- considering the mental health and wellbeing of your staff by listening to their concerns
- aiming to protect and mitigate the pressure staff are under by making necessary changes in your school culture

> This quote came from a Headteacher, who has been working on improving staff wellbeing in his school as a top priority. The following statement shows the epiphany he had about what staff wellbeing is all about:
>
>> Although, as school leaders, you can put great wellbeing initiatives in place for staff, the success of any work towards wellbeing, needs to be underpinned by systems and cultures which not only help wellbeing to thrive, but are the backbone of how they can exist in the first place. There are many aspects to ensure that this happens... clear roles, a coaching and collective approach and a move away from top-down practises, more of a research-based approach to any new ideas and initiatives to avoid knee-jerk and unsustainable ways of working, and a sense of braveness to stand firm against pressure to 'do things' just because there seems to be a trend to follow.

Ofsted (2019a) asked teachers for their views about how school leaders support with workload; stress and wellbeing and the findings were mixed:

> Senior leaders are seen to positively contribute to well-being by some. When this is the case, senior leaders support a positive work culture, are accessible to staff, listen to them, value them as professionals,

recognise their work and support their autonomy. In other cases, senior leaders are thought to contribute to low well-being. This is when there is poor communication with staff, an autocratic management style, workload pressure, and insufficient support and collaboration with staff. Addressing the issues would improve the workplace culture.

I am not proposing that you have an easy job as a school leader. I realise that you have a barrage of demands coming to you in quick succession every day from parents, children, staff or the government, for example, coordinating the organisation through the recent COVID-19 situation, which undoubtedly was an intense-pressure situation for you to manage. Although some teachers may place full responsibility on you as a school leader, responsibility lies with the individual teacher, too. Every school leader is not, and should not be expected to be, an expert in mental health and wellbeing. However, you should know the basics of wellbeing and be aware of ways to signpost staff to mental health support as part of your role. My suggestion is that, in order to assure the future long-term success of your school, a focus on teacher wellbeing is paramount; hopefully I have convinced you of this throughout my book so far, and the following information will be helpful so you can set some wheels in motion.

The Health and Safety Executive (HSE) (2019) identify six areas of risk that they call 'Management Standards'. These can be used by you when risk-assessing a staff member who gives you concern and when reflecting upon and ascertaining the cause of any work-related stress in your school. The Management Standards are:

- Demands – such as workload, work patterns and the work environment
- Control – how much say the staff member has in the way they do their work
- Support – the encouragement, sponsorship and resources provided by the school, senior leaders and colleagues
- Relationships – ways to avoid conflict, and dealing with unacceptable behaviour
- Role – whether people understand their role within the school and whether conflicting roles are not present
- Change – how change (large or small) is managed and communicated in the school

The Anna Freud National Centre for Children and Families (2019) reported that there are three types of wellbeing support that staff should receive. These are:

- specialist support, such as occupational health and an Employee Assistance Programme
- targeted support, such as training and wellbeing events
- universal support, such as having a teacher wellbeing policy, wellbeing drop-ins, a culture of no stigma of mental health issues and anonymous staff feedback about wellbeing

Why is a whole-school approach required?

Teacher wellbeing needs to be embedded in the ethos as a core value of the whole school. If sustained teacher wellbeing has yet to be established, then this desired change often has to come initially from the buy-in of a Headteacher. Although this change will ultimately benefit them, staff can show resistance to change. Change can be destabilising; some staff may fear change as it may have led to conflict in the past. Changes that are implemented in your school should be manageable and possible in real terms. It may be useful to ask yourself: how is change usually instigated? For example, does action happen from a top-down approach with school leaders initiating it, or via a bottom-up approach with ideas coming from less-senior staff?

- The Health Education Partnership (HEP, 2017:40) highlights that wellbeing is greatly influenced by the leadership of a school. They refer to a quote from the National Children's Bureau (2010) which specifies that,

Wellbeing is a manifestation of social justice, any model of human rights and an entitlement for all-but, at present, it is fragile and elusive for many.

The document *Supporting Staff Wellbeing in Schools* (Anna Freud National Centre for Children and Families and Schools in Mind, 2019:5—see Useful

Resources) lists the benefits that good whole-school staff wellbeing can have. These benefits illustrate to school leaders how a focus on teacher wellbeing is an investment for the future:

- Increased productivity of staff members.
- Reduced absences from work in relation to sickness (both short-term and long-term).
- Staff being able to manage stress better and develop healthier coping strategies.
- Improved job satisfaction, which can support retention.
- Staff feeling valued, supported and invested in.
- Positive impact on pupils, including improved educational outcomes, as both staff and children are more engaged.

An example of a whole-school staff wellbeing initiative, underpinned by the idea that when a school prioritises its staff wellbeing then pupils benefit, occurred in a grammar school: School leaders hosted an afternoon of wellbeing activities for teachers, including meditation and yoga classes, massage and breadmaking and didgeridoo workshops. These were all hosted by local businesses for no charge. One teacher commented:

> Teaching can be a stressful job, but if we are happy and relaxed then children are too, because they pick up on our vibes and moods.
>
> (Yorkshire Post, 2018).

Initiatives like this are useful but have low impact as one-off ventures.

All year-round wellbeing initiatives

An emphasis on teacher wellbeing needs to be constantly reinforced and upheld by the whole school. In Chapter 6, there is 'An Action Plan for School Leaders,' (Table 6.2), which details the necessary measures involved in working towards whole-school staff wellbeing. Schools need to respond to the symptoms of poor wellbeing, not the cause. A single day won't address or cure teacher wellbeing issues. Staff will see through feeble attempts to address teacher wellbeing with a 'tick-box' obligatory 'Staff Wellbeing Day' or a token gesture without any fervour on your part.

Here are some examples of ideas that may seem 'far-out' and unrealistic but worth consideration and would really show the promise of school leaders to address teacher wellbeing:

- *All staff to have their birthday off!:* This gesture of goodwill seems like a good idea but might be tricky to execute, for example, if a staff member's birthday is over a holiday, on a PPA day or on a training day. However, it may be possible to allow all staff to have one 'special day' off per academic year; the date being agreed by both parties. For whatever effort this exerts, you will get back 10-fold in staff motivation. Staff are very grateful if you provide a little flexibility. Staff may want to use their paid 'special day' to spend time with their family etc. In a similar vein, and if the 'special day' won't work for your school, consider whether it is viable for you to allow all staff to have half a day off each (either at the end of November or beginning of December) to do their Christmas shopping. I imagine this would be very gratefully received.

    On a separate note, I suggest that it is good practice to allow staff members to attend the funerals of close friends and relatives, despite what the local authority HR manual specifies.
- *A Golden Week for your staff:* This may only be every other month, or three times a year, but this will give your staff something to look forward to. Golden Week could be marked with, for instance, staff being instructed to leave by 4pm every day that week, or for all staff to enjoy a continental breakfast together every morning that week (from 8am until lessons start). If you wish to include a week of treats for your hardworking staff, then I suggest that you ask them for their ideas about how their 'Golden Week' can be realistically approached to suit them.
- Health care considerations: If free health care for staff is not viable due to financial constraints, consider offering free flu jabs for staff. If you are a large school, it may be possible for you to employ an HR manager so that an expert is on hand for any staff queries. Consider the Employee Assistant Programmes (EAPs) that you could provide for your staff to access.

A school's vision and environment

The school environment is an important factor for school leaders to consider when improving the levels of teacher wellbeing. Schools need to take ownership and make decisions, not from government advice, but with their own demographic and circumstances in mind. However, it should be stressed that it takes a brave leader to step outside of the norm. With the best will in the world, sometimes even a forward-thinking leader is not able to accomplish what they want, due to, for instance, governors not being in agreeance and having a narrow view of what impact is possible, or due to budget constraints.

The HEP paper (2017:40) describe the environment as:

> the school building, contents, surrounding grounds and how they look and appeal to the senses, such as proportions, scale, rhythm, light, materials, noise, temperature, odours and colours.

I recently visited a school that smelled strongly of urine; this made me consider the negative impact this may have on children and staff.

HEP suggest adding pleasant seating areas, plants and updating the staff room, if the budget allows, giving it a homely and relaxed feel.

Ofsted (2011:19) assert that 'hygiene, cleanliness and tidiness' should be given high priority by schools. Ofsted (2019a:3) state that:

> Staff perceive lack of resources as a problem that stops them from doing their job as well as they can.

This suggests that having a lack of supplies can lead to the frustration and the 'disempowerment' of teachers.

The HEP paper (2017) also mentions that a school environment comprises of psychosocial elements such as the attitudes and values of staff, children and parents as well as school procedures. They provide some examples of how schools involved in their project instigated a whole-school collective ethos:

- By creating a booklet of the school's core values for parents and carers.

- Every child and staff member wrote their hopes and dreams on a strip of paper that were all woven into a tapestry that was presented in the school's entrance.
- The unique values of a school were incorporated into every theme of the PSHE curriculum.

One value that a school can uphold is 'supporting wellbeing'. Once the value is agreed upon and shared, a school could explore the term 'wellbeing' and settle on pertinent areas of wellbeing to embed.

A school culture that respects and acknowledges staff wellbeing

Education is a human endeavour. The term 'education' means 'to mould', and so the values of compassion, empathy and nurturing need to be central to what teachers do. However, the toxic environment of some schools does nothing to support teacher wellbeing, and this environment can only be permanently changed at a whole-school level with the compliance of all staff.

Rogers (2012:8) claims that schools need to:

> build a supportive colleague culture that allows a confident sharing of concerns; that encourages colleagues to seek support; that allows honest professional discourse. It rarely happens naturally. It depends- in significant part- on the kind of leadership team within a given school.

This quote highlights the need for this kind of sharing to be factored into a school's teamwork planning. It is useful to avoid the habit of moaning and blaming others, and therefore, taking an autonomous approach to one's own wellbeing is key. It is rarely useful to form cliques within a staff team, even though this is in often in response to feeling a lack of control within a school. Rogers (2012:14) also specifies that stress and overwhelm can be 'moderated by a sense of shared collegial reality', where a shared sense of community, purpose and belonging underpins the work a staff team are doing.

As a school leader, it is crucial that you dedicate time to team-building and time for staff to work together on learning and teaching projects instigated from their passion or specialism. Giving staff the freedom and opportunity to spread their wings and develop initiatives they can be proud of with your support is integral to their wellbeing. Demonstrating professional trust towards your employees is important, for example, agreeing for them to work from home during their PPA time if this will allow them to achieve more. Giving teachers more autonomy, and avoiding micromanagement, lessens the chance of having demoralised staff.

The government document (2017) *Transforming children and young people's mental health provision: a green paper*, advocated having a designated mental health lead (DMHL) in schools; someone to oversee whole-school pupil and staff wellbeing. Be aware of the pressure that your staff are already under when you allocate this role, and ask yourself if you can feasibly add to that person's workload. In regard to staff wellbeing, the DMHL may gather feedback from staff regularly (maybe using an anonymous wellbeing comments box), organise social events for staff and arrange and organise coaching mentors, which leads to the next area of practice...

Peer coaching or mentoring for wellbeing

Much has been written lately about the value of peer coaching or mentoring in school, both for wellbeing benefits (like the wellbeing buddy system I mentioned in Chapter 3) and also for learning purposes, such as co-teaching and peer observation. This can be hard to manage among colleagues, however, due to personality clashes and differences in opinions and views. Perhaps you have reflected upon how this would work in your particular school. It may be that you have invested in an external coach or counsellor for your staff's wellbeing needs. Whatever the circumstances, the process needs to be supportive rather than judgmental and never used as a surveillance strategy.

Observations in schools can lead to a tremendous amount of stress and worry. O'Leary & Price (2016:114) write that 'Just the very mention of the word 'observation' can cause panic and trepidation.' They write about challenging the negative ideas that surround observations and state that being observed by a peer rather than your line manager has many positives. They also explore how not grading lessons often takes the fear out of observations.

O'Leary & Price (2016:115) describe peer observation as:

> a collaborative, often reciprocal, model of observation where peers get together to observe each other's practice. The observation is not regarded as an end in itself but as a springboard for sharing ideas and stimulating reflective dialogue.

I would like to see more of a power balance within the observational process in schools, and I think this would benefit teacher wellbeing. An example of such a structure would be:

1) Where the observee, in their wisdom, proposes the focus for observation according to what they feel is the area that need progression and attention.
2) The observation would comprise of the observer recording a log of the lesson (reserving any judgements at that stage) so that the lesson proceedings can be easily recalled afterwards.
3) Following the observation, a discussion with rich dialogue would be stimulated and positive learning would take place. In opposition to this, a negative observation may tell a teacher where they went wrong but may not focus on how they can improve. In other words, some observations weigh the pig but do nothing to fatten the pig—although please don't presume I'm referring to teachers as pigs!
4) A supportive observation would allow time for self-reflection, and a follow-up conversation would ensue, about a week later, where the observation process can be shared and impact measured. For example, conversations may focus on how worthwhile the observation was, if change has been instigated, and what are the next steps, if any.
5) If this process works well in your school, it could be further developed by forming triads, rather than pairs, thereby adding a third person who acts as a facilitator. This person can provide feedback, celebrate the positive aspects of the whole process and minimise any contention from occurring between parties.

Continued professional development (CPD)

CPD is important for staff wellbeing. Engaging in CPD helps teachers to stay motivated and inspired by their subject. It can boost passion for teaching in general. Ideally, the CPD offered to staff should be matched to the School Improvement Plan and have a wide range of training opportunities available so staff can explore and learn about an area that excites them.

If there is limited budget for training, then Future Learn (see Useful resources) has a variety of free online courses for staff to complete if time is given for this. The NHS advocate '5 ways to wellbeing' and emphasise the wellbeing impact of learning, so this should be promoted in schools. Morrison McGill, in his five-point plan (see Useful resources), specifies to:

> Invest more than £500 per member of staff per year for professional development. In fact, treble this to ensure there is scope for internal and external development and keep some cash spare for personal and professional classroom development; set by the teacher, not the appraiser.

A few years ago, my Head of School at university agreed for me to be trained as a Youth Mental Health First Aid Instructor; therefore, I am qualified to deliver the MHFA two-day course, which accredits participants as 'mental health first aiders'. This training had a very positive effect on me at work and significantly increased my wellbeing. It empowered me and made me feel as if my personal aspirations and my work-life were aligned.

Behaviour management as a top priority for leaders

Although it may be very challenging to address the behaviour in your school, it is crucial that school leaders:

> ...fully support teachers to implement behaviour policies consistently and ensure that the overall school culture helps to optimise pupils' behaviour,
>
> (Ofsted, 2019a:2).

Ofsted found that the 'perceived lack of support from senior managers, especially in managing pupils' behaviour' was explained as an 'inconsistent approach to managing behaviour' and 'a lack of parental support', too. This signifies that staff need to feel supported and empowered. The school's values and aspirations for behaviour management need to be agreed upon, clear and constantly reinforced. School leaders should be prepared and available to support with behavioural incidents and parental complaints rather than letting teachers deal with these alone. It is useful for school leaders to make their presence known around school, such as during lunchtime and on the playground.

An open dialogue in school around wellbeing

The most important change to make towards teacher wellbeing can be done very easily: you make mental health part of everyday conversations in your school because this normalises it. This can be very powerful in itself and can instigate massive change, although it may take time for this message to trickle down to everyone.

Secondly, it is important for all school leaders to have a focus on their own wellbeing needs and to role model and talk about their own self-care strategies, so staff know that it is a school priority. It is crucial that school leaders are not afraid of having difficult conversations, as avoiding such discussions often perpetuates the problem. As a school leader, though, you should not be expected to provide an 'open door' for staff to share their worries and concerns with you whenever they arise. It is understandable to value your privacy and to need a quiet, undisturbed office so you can concentrate. However, the clear acceptance from management that staff can talk about mental wellbeing reduces stigma and discrimination.

> A Headteacher once shared with me that the thing he was most proud about was that he never heard anything secondhand in his school. This shows that staff feel able to come to him immediately to voice any concerns or worries that they have.

This open dialogue, where staff are able to show their appreciation for each other and have regular appraisals where their feelings are acknowledged can be powerful in increasing teacher wellbeing. If you wish to go above and beyond in this area, then consider including a time slot in staff meetings to mention teacher wellbeing and to celebrate its success.

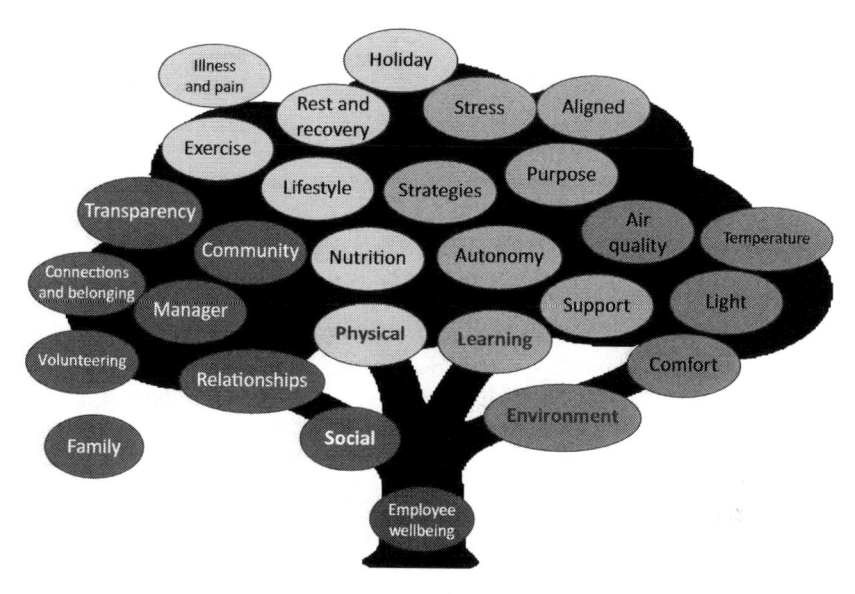

Figure 5.1 An example of an employee wellbeing tree.

> One school I visited began their conversations around wellbeing by all contributing ideas to an 'Employee wellbeing tree' that was displayed on the staffroom wall. Figure 5.1 below represents the finished product, although Post-It notes were available for staff to keep adding ideas throughout the year. Be mindful that these words are a personal representation of what employee wellbeing looks like to one specific school; your words may be very different.

Listening to the wellbeing concerns of staff

Learning how to listen to someone in mental health crisis is a skill that could come in handy in all aspects of your life. Just as physical first aid may save a life, knowing mental health first aid can do the same.

> I have undertaken basic counselling training and attended various crisis- and suicide-prevention courses, and without them, I am not sure how I would have coped with encountering a young girl who wanted to jump from a motorway bridge on a cold November morning. I was extremely grateful for my training at that moment and found

that the simple guidance I had learnt helped me to bring her to safety. It might help you to know about how I approached this difficult situation, and what I learnt about supporting a deeply disturbed and scared person:

I was driving to a school, where a student teacher was waiting for me to observe her lesson, when I noticed a hunched over figure at a bridge by the side of the road. I continued driving but I became increasingly uneasy about what I'd seen. At the next roundabout I turned back to check on this person. I approached a young woman who was visibly upset and appeared to be holding a tissue as she leaned over (I later found out that she was clasping her suicide note). My first sentence to her was 'This is none of my business, but I just wanted to check that you're okay? Are you thinking of jumping?' She replied, 'Yes, I want to die'.

So, do you know how you would react to this situation? What would your next words be to this young girl?

Telling her not to jump may be your first instinct, but this is not what I said. I gently responded, 'Sounds like you're feeling really desperate, sweetie. What's happening for you today?' Perhaps you would have found asking her if she felt suicidal an uncomfortable question. I have learnt that asking whether someone in a mental health crisis is suicidal is a very important thing to do. Contrary to common belief, asking this will not put the idea of suicide in their head; it will allow them to express their feelings of desperation. I made sure that I did not show judgement and tried all I could to show empathy, focusing on exploring her feelings and trying to instil feelings of hope were my goals here. I made two mistakes, though, and asked about her family and friends and whether I could call anyone. She said that her family and friends don't care. At times she got quite aggressive and told me to leave her alone. I stayed, calmly rubbing her back and telling her it was understandable that she was feeling this way. I asked her whether she had any pets and she said that she used to have a dog she loved very much but her parents had made her give him away. Thinking of injecting hope into her mind I asked her age, and when she answered that she was 17, I said that when she was a bit older and had her own place to live, she could have as many dogs as she wanted. This made her smile weakly.

Next, I witnessed how powerful my lived experience was and how my acceptance of her feelings impacted her in a positive way. My counselling training taught me to keep the focus on the person I was helping and not to bring my own feelings into the interaction, so I was cautious. Usually, active listening skills (which I will cover later in this chapter) involve not reverting the focus to yourself but keeping within the

> person's frame of reference without your own feelings encroaching. Nevertheless, I realised that I could tell her that, in a small way, I understood her desire to die and end her suffering; it was only when I talked about my own desperately low point (wanting to die myself) that she stopped crying, listened and looked me in the eyes and told me that knowing that made her feel less lonely. The disclosure of my own suffering instigated a discussion about how she could possibly start rebuilding her life and search for some joy again, like I had; I assured her that there is always hope, regardless of how bad you feel in the moment. She then implored, 'Do you feel better? Do you still feel like you want to die?' If you want to find out how this story ends, then I will share it in Chapter 6.

Disclosing your own struggles with mental health as a school leader, or talking about someone close to you, may allow one of your staff to feel an acceptance about admitting to their own. When this happens, this is their first step towards becoming well again. Discussing your own feelings about mental health will not make you appear weak. It will show your strength, humility and humanity.

> Here is a quote from a Headteacher who shared his personal history with staff and noticed a shift in attitudes:
>
> When we decided to start to unpick the topic of staff wellbeing and mental health in school, I felt that it was essential to set the scene as to why it was so important. On a training day focussing on the topic, I used the Mental Health at Work report (2016), which was current at the time. I used data from that report to prompt discussion, but I also wanted staff to see why I was so driven to address the issue. For that reason, I shared my own experience of clinical depression from several years before. I said that I had sought help, had medication and counselling; I could see from the reaction on people's faces that there was an important change in how they saw me. After the session and at the end of the day, staff came to me to thank and praise me for being so open. I also had emails telling me how good the day was because of the openness. I felt that staff felt more confident that I would understand any issues they had and indeed, combined with my MHFA qualification, several staff approached me directly with issues. Being open certainly didn't demonstrate weakness; in fact, it was seen as the complete opposite.

The ESP reported in the 'Teacher Wellbeing Index' (2019:9) that:

> ...60% of educational professionals would not feel confident in disclosing unmanageable stress/mental health issues to their employer.

This shows that depending upon a variety of factors, a teacher who is experiencing wellbeing issues may or may not feel able to approach you for support. Here is a brief summary of the best way to approach this:

- *When a staff member comes to you:* If a staff member comes to you and discloses a wellbeing issue, then listen to them and promise confidentiality, except where issues pose a health and safety risk to either themselves or others. The use of active listening skills shows your care and concern for someone. A relaxed and open posture is important and plenty of eye contact (but not staring). You may like to paraphrase and summarise to check on the person's true meaning, for example, 'It sounds as if… am I correct? I'm hearing that… is that how you feel?' Remember that you are not a mental health expert, and so it is not in your remit to diagnose; you merely need to be open-minded and accepting of whatever your staff member is feeling. Ask them if they are aware of any external wellbeing resources or services and ask how these could be accessed by them. It is obviously difficult to allow staff to use a service in the school day, but these kind-of conversations can open up the dialogue around wellbeing.
- *When a staff member doesn't come to you:* If you perceive a potential problem with one of your staff but they have not come to talk to you about this, then tread gently. You may have noticed a pattern of absence or erratic behaviour. Be aware that they may not even recognise what's happening to them. Always avoid the teacher faux pas of treating adults like children. The staff member may also pretend they are alright or may feel too anxious about seeking help. Catching a colleague's dip in wellbeing early gives them the best chance to get help, however, broaching the subject may be difficult. Choose a private space to talk to the staff member and keep a non-judgmental and accepting manner. Reassure them that your motive in speaking to them is supportive rather than to chastise. Try to establish the main cause of their stress. Consider whether

you can adapt certain tasks or work environments that are contributing to their distress. You are required, under the Equality Act 2010, to make 'reasonable adjustments' for a worker who is struggling with their mental health. Ask them about previous wellbeing coping strategies that have worked for them and encourage these. Ask the staff member to describe their specific feelings in response to their stress rather than labelling it as 'stress'; this is because the term 'stress' is subjective. Focusing on the feelings behind one's stress is more useful than labelling it. It is important to be sensitive about what the person is able to cope with in that moment. If they are in the midst of a crisis, they may not be thinking logically or be able to take all the information in. Therefore, it may be necessary to write notes of the conversation accurately to remind you and the teacher of your interaction, especially if you both agree to work towards specific goals. Try to reassure them that their job is safe and that support will be available for them, either internally to the school or externally.

It may help you to memorise the following structure or conversational stages to go through as the acronym VERSE:

- *Value the rapport* you can build with the teacher by working on allowing them to feel comfortable, safe and trusting of you before you talk about how they are.
- *Explore* how they are feeling using active-listening skills (more details at the end of this chapter).
- *Risk-assess* their situation. Think of the mental health continuum for teachers (Chapter 2) and where they currently are on this scale. If you sense they are feeling suicidal, ask them about this. There is a section in Chapter 6 about how to deal with staff in crisis.
- Ask them about *Strategies* that have helped them in the past. Identify what they see as needing to happen. Ask directly what you can do in your role to help them. Putting the onus on them helps you to personalise their support and encourage autonomy. If they are not in a fit state to think, then make your own suggestions and gauge their reaction.
- *End* the conversation warmly and recap and review what has been discussed.

Making all staff feel seen, heard and cared for

The practice of regularly checking-in with your staff cannot be understated. From teacher wellbeing workshops I've delivered, the overriding message I've gained is that teachers want to feel noticed by school leaders. This often just takes a sincere 'how are you today?' as you walk around school. Making your staff feel appreciated will minimise and avoid a culture of 'presentee-ism'. This attitude will encourage staff productivity and increase job satisfaction, as staff feel they are making a difference and their hard work is being acknowledged.

Step 10: Expressing gratitude and acknowledging staff

There are a number of ways you can express your gratitude, for example:

- Write notes/emails that deliver your personal appreciation.

    I know of a Headteacher who bought a chocolate bar for each of his staff at the beginning of half term as a 'Thank Crunchie it's half-term' gesture. Each chocolate bar had a sentence (on a Post-It note) that related to one thing they had done for the school which he valued and was grateful for.

- Verbally praise the work of individual teachers in meetings and disseminate this to governors, parents etc.

When I deliver a pedagogy session to the trainee teachers at university, often the resounding message within every lesson is the importance of knowing individual children to be able to support their pastoral and academic needs effectively. This is true also for school leaders; the most essential element of a good manager is to know your staff well and subsequently know how to treat them. If you know your staff well, then it will be easy for you to spot the signs that their wellbeing is suffering and that they appear to be acting differently to the norm. Organising a one-to-one meeting with staff occasionally means that you can interact in a quality way with each member of staff.

> *When the Head of Department joined our team, she made certain to have a 'one-to-one' with every staff member. Although this must have been a logistical nightmare, and a strain on her time when she had so much to get to grips with, we fully appreciated her effort; it showed us that it mattered to her to get to know us all individually.*

Tips for school leaders to keep unnecessary pressure off teachers

- Don't push initiatives on your staff without considering the negative impact on them. Try to lessen the power balance in the quality-assessing systems you use, for example, rather than announcing a book scrutiny or trawl at a moment's notice, have a session during a staff meeting where everyone brings books and discuss on an informal basis.
- Ask yourself whether paperwork or workload can be simplified to avoid burden. For example, have quick-start guides for your school policies that are displayed on just a single page so that workload is reduced for teachers and student teachers. Encourage teachers to provide verbal feedback to pupils and AFL to limit the marking required outside of a lesson. In addition, limit the written detail required in reports to parents. Restricting report content to a few short but quality statements will avoid overwhelming parents and probably make it more likely that they will take key points on board.

> After over 20 years of parent's evenings, I have concluded that most parents want to know if their child is happy at school, if they are behaving well, if they have friends and their child's basic attainment in core subjects. In my experience, parents tended to ask what their child's strengths were, and what work they should focus on at home to support their child further; all this information could be shared in a very succinct way.

- Avoid staff meetings situations where one or two people dominate the proceedings and leave other staff wondering why they are there. This diminishes the value of future meetings. Therefore, make the aims and purpose of each meeting clear. Try to limit the frequency and length of meetings so they do not become habitual but are planned for a particular purpose. Avoid the circling of issues within meetings by being decisive when this is required. In addition, it is important to thank the staff for attending meetings and for their contributions. Simple things like this go a long way and allows staff to feel that you have noticed their commitment and hard work.

Here are two real-life examples of good practice in schools where school leaders are prioritising staff wellbeing:

A spotlight on St John's Middle School Academy

St John's Middle School Academy is at the beginning of their journey to address teacher wellbeing. However, the senior leadership team are devoted and optimistic that they can plan for personal and effective provision, so that staff have the optimal wellbeing required to meet the demands and challenges of 21st century teaching. School leaders recognise that teacher wellbeing is central to the school's success and that they are accountable and have a moral responsibility to create the best conditions and environment to enable their teachers to thrive.

The school motto is 'Give of Your Best', and this is certainly true for how teacher wellbeing is being approached thus far; school leaders wish to protect staff from the constantly changing external educational demands, especially in relation to workload and Ofsted. Their long-term goals include the completion of a staff wellbeing policy and strategies that staff can draw from, such as Wellness Action Plans from Mind (see Useful resources).

Teacher wellbeing initiatives

To date, they have:

- Organised extended twilight training to limit staff meetings. The twilights include a buffet to thank staff for their attendance.
- Dedicated twilight sessions for a teacher wellbeing workshop and a social and wellbeing activity.
- Allowed staff to request time off to attend health appointments or to watch their children's school plays etc.
- Purchased five wellbeing books for staff to borrow. This was instigated and ordered by the Executive Head.
- Made plans to have five trained mental health first aiders (MHFA England) in their school in the next six months.

A personal approach to wellbeing

School leaders understand that to keep staff happy and to secure staff retention, they need to comprehend exactly what wellbeing means to all staff; they appreciate the importance of consulting with everyone before making any decisions. I delivered a wellbeing workshop

Figure 5.2 An example of what wellbeing means to the staff at St John's Middle School Academy.

in 2019 at St John's and asked staff what the term 'teacher wellbeing' meant to them (Figure 5.2).

What is staff wellbeing to us?

The results show a range of ideas which will be used to inform plans for teacher wellbeing in the school by forming a wellbeing working group to start discussions…

Wellbeing working group

They have formed a wellbeing working group that consists of staff that are passionate about mental health and wellbeing. The working group reflects the wider school community, including governors. Within this working group, they are currently formulating a staff survey to gauge the current levels of wellbeing amongst staff and to obtain a good evidence-base to work from. Outcomes of the survey will be analysed and presented, and key themes will be identified that inform the whole-school wellbeing priorities, actions and resources. This survey will come with a rationale letter that explains to staff what their unique mission is: to build resilience in their teachers who frequently deal with 'safeguarding, behavioural and emotional challenges'. They acknowledge that staff need 'the appropriate support, understanding and professional development' in order to cope with increasing pressures.

The lead of the wellbeing working group has a goal to encourage colleagues to gain the skill of emotional self-regulation. She intends to use the model of Maslow's hierarchy of needs (1943) and apply the knowledge of psychology to drive the wellbeing work forward. She wishes to be regarded as a caring employer and to develop a proactive response, rather than a reactive response, to teacher wellbeing.

A spotlight on Kempsey Primary School Academy
'We are family!'

The staff at Kempsey Primary School work as a close team. They are family to each other. The usual dynamics that are expected of a family unit are at play, with all the joys and the frustrations, but at the core, they are all about caring for each other. They may not be formally engaged in peer support, but the practices of encouragement and championing of each other happen daily. Staff feel seen and heard, and the Headteacher makes sure of this, at both a collective and individual level.

At the root of all education, there should be a significant emphasis on care and nurturing. This Headteacher realises that teachers need attention, time to reflect and to have their feelings listened to and acknowledged if they are expected to care for children and cope with the pressured situations involved in their jobs. This is what she provides, unconditionally with her ready sense of humour and humility. She did concede that, of course, it is in her best interests to look after her staff because, at a mercenary level, if she doesn't, then she risks staff absence due to stress.

Our conversation about teacher wellbeing steered towards the importance of a teacher role-modelling good wellbeing to their class and sharing with honesty how they are feeling each day. One teacher at Kempsey Primary admitted that she had been crying before a lesson and an observant child had asked her if she was okasy. She had admitted to this child that she had been feeling upset. Real face-to-face human connection is lacking in many of the activities young people engage in, such as gaming and social media. Therefore, if a teacher can be brave enough to be open and truthful about how they are feeling (within reason), then they are role modelling the fact that we are all human and all have the capacity to feel sadness, pain and loss. I am certain that many of the children in this school have witnessed staff members look after each other, role-model self-care strategies and show the emotional resilience necessary to deal with the ups and downs of a demanding teaching role. In fact, in just one week, children would have been privy to a staff massage day (where each person was allocated a 20 minute massage slot) and also aware of the Headteacher's treat to buy, prepare and serve all the staff a bacon roll as a thank you. This in itself shows the pupils that self-care and relaxation is part of wellbeing, and that looking after each other and appreciating others is key to good relationships.

Wellbeing initiatives

There has been a strong focus on staff wellbeing for many years at Kempsey Primary School. The Headteacher understands that in order for staff to work at their best, their wellbeing has to be at its best. The following initiatives are consistently weaved into school provision:

- Staff massage every half term (this has been running for six years now).
- Golden Week where staff leave at 3.30pm every day.
- Birthday fairy—where everyone puts their names in a hat and has a gift on their special day.
- A counsellor is paid for by the school to see staff every fortnight; this is soon to become weekly.
- Virtual training days have been added so that staff can work at home and still engage with training, albeit remotely.
- They have a Staff Wellbeing Day as part of the School Trust alliance, which takes place on a Monday (so staff can have a long weekend) in November and all four schools shut. Staff have the day for Christmas shopping or relaxing. One teacher enjoyed a spa day.
- They have a TA Appreciation Day where teaching assistants have a day off; the rationale behind this is for staff to see first-hand how lucky they are to have a TA in their class.
- A therapy dog, called Erik, visits once a week for children and staff. Staff meet up regularly in their own time to walk their dogs together.
- The Headteacher enables staff to visit the doctors during school time if required.
- After the Ofsted inspection, the governors have funded a meal for all staff to celebrate. Governors also write letters to staff once a year praising them for the contributions they have made.

Challenges to teacher wellbeing: Parents and Ofsted

Two teachers from the school admitted that their wellbeing is sometimes rocked when they experience a lack of trust from parents and that this is the time when they most appreciate the Headteacher. They described how the headteacher always gives her complete support and backs staff, which allows them to feel safe and protected. Ofsted reported that a strength to the leadership of the school was the protection of staff. Surely the feeling of safety is one, if not the most, key element to someone's wellbeing.

When I enquired about what challenges they face in ensuring that staff wellbeing is in place, Ofsted featured as the main perpetrator. Words and phrases used by teachers to describe the inspection experience were: 'horrific', 'hostile', 'feeling beaten into the ground' and 'it broke me completely'. Despite the high staff wellbeing and collegial atmosphere of this school, the Headteacher could do nothing to protect her staff from the bombardment of Ofsted. The whole process, to them, felt like an unfair fight and that overall, there was nothing affirming about the experience. They described it as 'combative' and 'gruelling'. They admitted that waiting for the results was excruciating and although the outcome was good for them, it was disappointing and disheartening that the inspection ended with the passing over of a generic report that lacked a true representation of the school and failed to capture its very essence. The damage to staff from an Ofsted visit in a school more fragmented than this, and with less synergy, I fear would be massive.

Next steps for Kempsey's staff wellbeing

Staff are in talks about developing a staff wellbeing policy, and they are creating a proforma for this led by the DMHL, who is an extremely empathetic and intuitive teacher. She seeks the guidance of the school counsellor to provide her with expert advice about mental health and wellbeing. The school plan to add a 'wellbeing teacher target' to the performance management process. The dedication and commitment of the senior leaders in this school is exemplary. Spending time in this environment even makes me want to return to teaching, if only for the hugs and warm, friendly atmosphere that is so very conducive to my wellbeing. There is the feeling that, as a team, they are infallible and cling together against all odds. The bedrock of the school, that withstands educational storms and change, are the human values that are apparent in the staff. The Headteacher allows staff the chance to express themselves honestly and cry in her office if they need to. If all teachers had this opportunity and the buffer, support and protection (in the Headteacher's words, to get their 'head straight' in her office), then I am adamant that there would be better teacher wellbeing in our schools. Teachers, in order to stay well, need acceptance, the chance to let out their feelings and acknowledgement; this Headteacher offers all three in spades.

How staff can support their school leader

If you have hardworking and empathic school leaders like those I've described above, then it's important to appreciate them and realise the work they put in (for instance phoning tricky parents and dealing with the most challenging pupil behaviour). Remember to thank school leaders if they support your wellbeing, and show your appreciation for their care and concern.

A stronger focus is needed on the wellbeing of school leaders. Our current school system places the responsibility and emphasis of teacher wellbeing onto school leaders, which seems altogether unfair. It leaves me imploring: who is looking out for our school leaders?

The ESP (2019) 'Teacher Wellbeing Index', surveying 1187 staff, found that 84% of school leaders described themselves as 'stressed'. One recommendation in the 'Teacher Wellbeing Index' (2019:77) was 'All senior leaders should have access to personal and peer support. Tackling the level of chronic stress reported among this group should be made a priority.' This indicates that the wellbeing of a school leader is not being considered sufficiently within education as it stands.

These quotes from Headteachers exemplify how some school leaders may feel:

> *All day I have teachers, staff and children coming to me. They tell me their problems. I have staff shortages and safeguarding matters that mount up. I have parental issues. Everything feels as if it's the senior leadership team's fault. On some days, it feels like I am viewed by everyone as a machine without feelings, as no one considers me. Staff just see wellbeing as a teacher issue and something for senior leaders to sort out; the wellbeing of senior leaders is forgotten. What they don't see is that we are protecting them from messages we're hearing that we have to drip-feed to staff so they don't panic, for example, changes to the Ofsted framework. I have my family to turn to and I would visit my GP if I was feeling really bad, but I know that I have to be seen as a strong figure head to everyone at school.*

> *You have to set the tone and look after others. You cannot be vulnerable yourself. I've always thought that staff have to have confidence in my leadership and know that I am strong and won't let them down. I'm lucky that I have some very empathic and intuitive*

> staff, and this helps. I have our MAT's Chief Finance Officer, who I feel is someone that I can go to and share my feelings with. There will be cards on my desk from staff, or someone will pick up on how I am feeling and show consideration. I feel a shared commonality with some members of staff who have been through similar difficult experiences to me and that helps. However, I find it hard, as it is a little bit one-sided and I don't always get appreciation.

Tips for school leaders to minimise their own pressure (using the acronym 'SWIM')

- *Safeguard your time*: Read my section on procrastination and guard yourself against wasting time. Control interruptions on your time by having a sign that you can put on your door that says 'Please don't disturb' when it is vital that you need to concentrate and focus. If you are interrupted by a staff member, try in a friendly way to keep the conversation on point and avoid small talk. Remain standing if you have limited time; this will signify that you are busy. Give them your undivided attention in that moment, but if the discussion continues beyond the time you have available, arrange a meeting at a more convenient time. You may want to meet somewhere other than your office (unless it sounds like a confidential or sensitive issue), as this will allow you to leave when you feel the matter has been addressed.
- *Waive responsibility*: Give yourself a break when it comes to your staff's wellbeing because you won't be able to get it right for everyone. Try not to take criticisms personally, as often they are protesting the system rather than your ability as a Head, and you are powerless to change most bureaucracy.
- *Invest in your staff*: Passing on jobs that will motivate certain staff and encourage them to take on responsibility for an area they are passionate about is often a win-win situation, especially if training or professional development opportunities are offered alongside this. When you receive a new task, get in the habit of either acting on it, delegating it, filing it or deleting it, if this is appropriate. There is a skill to delegating, but it is important not to overload your staff with inappropriate tasks for their grade.

- *Model wellbeing:* I urge school leaders to take responsibility for their own wellbeing and admit that they are not invincible. As I've mentioned, try to model the behaviours that you'd like to see in others and show that having a work-life balance is sustainable.

A survey by the National Association of Headteachers has found that 34% of Heads are leaving before retirement (Ferguson, 2019). Ferguson interviewed Headteachers who had changed careers and asked them about their decisions. Utton, who is now an osteopath, said he:

> watched a number of friends die from stress, have nervous breakdowns or be booted out of the profession thanks to stupid decisions by Ofsted.

Another ex-Head, Thomas, commented that 'leaving teaching literally saved my life'.
He explained:

> I was working long hours. That put pressure on my marriage, and I didn't have time for my own children's school meetings, concerts or sports days. I started sleeping badly. I wasn't exercising; I wasn't eating well; I wasn't looking after myself.

He was only 50 but decided to leave his Headship and put his family and himself first and worked his way back to health. Before making the decision to quit, Heads should have support, but where?

Where should school leaders turn to for support?

It's all well and good to urge school leaders to consider the wellbeing of teachers in their school, but who is looking out for them? I have predicted the sources of support available to a school leader if their wellbeing dips:

The Chair of Governors?

The governors of a school can provide support to the school leaders if there are good relationships formed and trust established. It may be that a school leader feels able to share the difficulties they are facing within their professional boundaries and the stresses within the job role with their governing body, but not comfortable to share anything of a personal nature with them.

The Executive Head?

Again, this relies on the type of relationship that exists and levels of trust. Some school leaders, I imagine, wish to keep their personal and private lives separate. Some may feel that exposing their low feelings will cause judgement and that their line manager's opinion will be that they are 'not coping'. However, if a supportive relationship exists, then this could be a helpful person for a school leader to turn to for guidance. Often, Executive Headteachers and the governing body have support mechanisms within their own teams. An Executive Head may also meet with other headteachers that they have built connections with, for instance, at conferences, and this can prove a good source of support.

The school's counsellor?

Some schools are lucky enough to have a counsellor designated to work with pupils. Often, there is the opportunity for staff to seek support from the counsellor, which could be useful for some school leaders. However, those that wish to keep work and private issues personal may not seek help in this way.

The Education Support Partnership?

I share the details of this charity throughout this book (see Useful resources). It was set up by experienced educational workers. Their website states:

> Sometimes work (or just life) can be tough. That's why we offer free, confidential help and support, no matter what your problem.

This service offers support via telephone or email and may be useful for a school leader in a time of need and to offer objective advice.

The other members of the Senior Leadership Team (SLT)?

It is useful to have built up, and made explicit, a support mechanism within an SLT. Therefore, everyone will have someone to approach if they need to offload or seek confidential advice. Again, this is dependent on relationships and relies upon the SLT having close connections and an affiliation with at least one other person on the team. It can work well in that the members of SLT may have gone through the same ranks as each other; therefore, they may have a shared understanding of the types of pressure involved. There is less chance of a school leader feeling that their ability at work is being questioned or scrutinised than if they went to their Executive Head, perhaps.

Within this kind of support mechanism, the onus is on the person feeling heard and their feelings being acknowledged. This type of debriefing conversation can go a long way in settling a person's angst. There should not be the expectation that your support colleague can solve anything for you, or else that risks building extra pressure for that member of staff.

Step 11: A support network for a school leader

If you refer back to my tips about how a school leader approaches a teacher experiencing low wellbeing, them much of that advice applies here—remember the acronym VERSE.

So it seems that the process of peer support is the most significant answer here to address and support a school leader's wellbeing. However, I would urge County Councils, Local Education Authorities and the DfE to look at how supervision and allocated professional support or workshops can be put in place for all staff in schools, but particularly for school leaders.

Supervision

If you compare the support a teacher receives to a counsellor, then the provision that is organised to support the wellbeing of a teacher appears negligible. A counsellor receives supervision that is paid for by their employer or workplace so that their mental health can be supported in response to the responsibility and emotional impact of their job. This supervision involves counselling to discuss feelings and triggers that have arisen during sessions with clients. Teachers can feel emotionally and physically drained, stressed by the accountability of their jobs, however, there are often minimal strategies put in place to deal with this overwhelm. This can lead to feelings of loneliness, especially if there is a culture of 'putting up or shutting up' in their school, or if staff feel that if they admit to feeling overwhelmed, then they will be judged negatively by the school's management.

The Anna Freud National Centre for Children and Families, in *Supporting Staff Wellbeing in Schools* report (2019) (see Useful resources), emphasises the need for teachers to be given supervision so they can discuss challenging and difficult areas of their work. They specify that:

> one of the key benefits/aims of supervision is that it reduces the feeling of being alone in managing a problem. Isolation can cause a great deal of work stress if someone feels as if they are carrying something on their own
>
> (2019:10).

A movement for good and a force for innovation in education is the Carnegie School of Education, which is part of Leeds Beckett University. In development with Talking Heads, they have created a National Hub for Supervision in Education, which offers:

> a range of professional learning programmes to help senior leaders to establish and develop a culture of supervision for teaching and pastoral staff.

The network of accredited supervisors can offer support to education professionals via Skype, face-to-face meetings or through peer groups (see Useful resources).

Useful resources

- The website https://www.countrysideclassroom.org.uk/resources provides staff and children with some useful ideas to improve the outside area of a school.
- For more information about values-based education, please visit http://www.valuesbasededucation.com/
- This useful guide by Morrison McGill provides you with a five-point plan for teacher wellbeing: https://www.teachertoolkit.co.uk/2014/07/03/5-point-plan-for-teacher-wellbeing/

- The charity, Education Support Partnership, offers help and support for anyone working in education.
  Phone: 0800 0562 561 (Freephone, 24 hours a day, 7 days a week)
  Text: 07903 341229
  Email: support@edsupport.org.uk
  Website: www.Educationsupportpartnership.org.uk/chat-support
- National Hub for Supervision in Education can be found at https://www.leedsbeckett.ac.uk/carnegie-school-of-education/national-hub-for-supervision-in-education/
- Mates in Mind produced a document about how line managers can talk to their staff about mental health; here is a link to it: https://www.matesinmind.org/assets/uploads/Lets_Talk_Lets_Act__Managers_Guide___Time_to_Talk_Day_2020__2.pdf
- Mind, *How to support staff who are experiencing a mental health problem* (Resource 4), Available at: www.mind.org.uk/work

Takeaway message: What are active listening skills?

Active listening takes focus and concentration. If you are listening to another member of staff and you want to show them empathy and 'unconditional positive regard' (Rogers, 1951, as cited in McLeod, 2014), you need to be aware of not only what they are saying but their tone of voice and body language. According to Mehrabian (1981), we communicate only 7% of what we say using words, 38% from the tone of our voice and 55% from our body language.

There are three things to consider when actively listening, shown as AAA:

- Attention—It is easy to lose track and start thinking about our own responses and our own agenda rather than paying attention when someone is speaking. However, we are only actively listening when our attention is fully on the other person in the moment. Before a meeting when you wish to actively listen, you may want to write the word 'listen' at the top of a piece of paper as a reminder. An anagram of 'listen' is 'silent', and knowing that often reminds me to be quiet when I'm tempted to talk too much (rather than listen), turn a conversation around to myself or become distracted by my own thoughts.

- Attitude—Having a non-judgmental and open attitude is key to listening effectively using a positive approach. It can be very powerful to temporarily shelve your own frame of reference and try to intuitively step into someone else's shoes and try to 'feel' the world from their perspective.
- Adjust—Try to remain flexible and don't assume how someone feels. Avoid the temptation to drive the conversation in your direction, but try to allow the person to explore at their pace; when I trained in counselling, my tutor would tell us to pretend that we were a passenger in the car and that the client was in the driver's seat. Continually check in to the meaning of what someone is saying, for example, by saying 'I'm hearing…is this how you feel?' This gives them a chance to agree or explain their thinking accurately to you.

Active listening is a skill but one that has great merit in allowing colleagues, or anyone in your life, to feel listened to and understood.

6

WHAT IS MY PERSONAL PLAN FOR WELLBEING?

Steps to success

This part of the book is for you to record your answers to Steps 1–11. You may have been completing the steps as you read each chapter, but if not now is your chance to reflect upon each step and list (in the 'notes' section provided) any related targets you might have to improve your overall wellbeing. You should also be celebrating those areas of wellbeing that you feel confident in. For example, you may have developed a regular habit of 'checking in' to your body and mind during your teaching days but still not achieved a work-life balance. This is your chance to go back over each chapter and use any of the signposts I have included in the 'Useful resources' sections and create a personal plan for how to proceed (Table 6.1).

- An action plan for school leaders

    Although most of the content within the below template (Table 6.1) has been covered already in this book, it has been created to give you,

158 A PERSONAL PLAN FOR WELLBEING

Table 6.1 Steps to success

Related sections of the book/Steps	Question to reflect upon	Your notes	Any related actions/targets/celebrations
Introduction **Step 1: Check-in to your wellbeing and take breaks**	Do I need to develop in self-awareness by checking in to my body and mind? If yes, when will I do this during the day? (e.g. morning and afternoon break, lunchtime and on the journey home) What questions will I ask myself about my mental and physical health during the day? For example: • Does my mind feel cluttered or does it feel spacious? • Can I detect any irritation in my mind and can I let go of this easily? • Are my thought processes fluid or do they feel blocked? • Have I got negativity and tension in my mind? At the same time, it is useful to assess your physical health by asking yourself questions such as: • Does my scalp feel tight? • Are my shoulders tense and stiff? How can I plan to incorporate more breaks into my teaching day? Can I work with a colleague so that we can enable each other to have small periods of non-contact time away from my class on a regular basis?	Write down any details about when, where and how you will 'check-in'…	
Chapter 1 **Step 2:** **Previous wellbeing strategies**	Can I list the strategies that I have used to support my wellbeing in the past? Why do I think these worked for me personally?	As you find other wellbeing strategies within this book that you wish to try, note them down in this section as a reminder…	
Step 3: **Learn to say 'no'**	Can I learn to say 'no' more? Can I, in a respectful way, say 'no' to a demand being placed on me at work this week and see how it feels?	Write about your experience of saying 'no'…	

WHAT IS MY PERSONAL PLAN FOR WELLBEING 159

Chapter 2

Step 4: Analysing fear and panic

If you experience anxiety, ask yourself: What is the main thing (or things) that I fear?

If you experience depression, ask yourself: What are the main things making me this sad?

Try to formulate a list of factors that may contribute to the anxiety or depression. Consider speaking to either a professional, your GP or a close friend or family member. If you are able to identify the precipitating factors of your anxiety or depression, this may lead you to a clear understanding of how to treat it in the best way.

Step 5: Stop and drop negative thoughts

Do I experience negative thoughts frequently? If yes, then apply the following:

When you notice and experience a string of negative thoughts during the day (you may recognise these during a check-in—see Step 1), say 'stop' and 'drop', then direct some loving thoughts towards yourself. Perhaps you can think of some simple affirmations that you can use to divert your attention and mind to a more positive place, e.g. every day in every way I am trying my best etc.

As you read the sections in this book about anxiety and/or depression, write down anything that may help you….

Write notes about how you will combat any negative thoughts…

Chapter 3

Step 6: Adding more pleasurable pursuits to your life

Can I think of anything that I can add to my life so I gain more resilience? E.g. a new hobby that empowers me and gives my life more meaning, or an activity I can partake in that is out of my comfort zone.

By looking at Figure 3.1 for ideas, see if you can add two extra things to your life that will give you added pleasure and life satisfaction. Plan an appropriate time to engage in these activities and try your best to fit them into your life.

Can you list at least six things that already enrich your life that are not connected to your work-life? Can you reflect on what positive elements each of these pastimes offer you?

(Continued)

Table 6.1 Continued

Related sections of the book/Steps	Question to reflect upon	Your notes	Any related actions/targets/celebrations
Step 7: Audit your time	Which of these tasks take over the most of my time? How much time do I spend engaging in the following activities each working week? • Teaching • Marking and assessment • Lesson preparation and classroom organisation • Non-teaching contact with pupils/parents • Meetings/training or management activities • Administrative tasks • Travelling to work • Sleeping • Eating • Hobbies/interests/leisure Reflect on the following questions after completing the audit: • Which of these were of most and least value to children? • Which if these gave me the most and least professional satisfaction? • Which of these caused me the most stress and frustration?	In order to gauge whether you have a work-life balance, it could be worth auditing the approximate time you spend over an average working week (Monday to Friday) engaging in certain tasks. If you are part-time, then audit only the workdays. These audits may be tricky to complete if you spend a lot of time multitasking as many teachers do! In addition, it is hard to find an average week in teaching, as each week can be very different in a school. Write down any notes here about the audits you complete. Jot down any strategies from Chapter 3 that you can incorporate to give you more of a work-life balance...	

WHAT IS MY PERSONAL PLAN FOR WELLBEING   161

Chapter 4

Step 8: No one is perfect!

Am I able to diplomatically admit that I do not know something to a child in my class or to a parent? If not, why?

Do I forgive myself for the things that do not go as planned during the teaching day? Can I 'let go' of these things and put them down to experience that I will learn from? After all, it has been said that 'you don't make mistakes, mistakes make you'.

For this step, I wish for you to deliberate upon whether perfectionism in teachers serves or disadvantages their wellbeing. I would also like you to consider if you ever demonstrate perfectionism within your teaching persona.

Go through these ideas below and if you are a perfectionist, note down the changes you can make:

Solutions to perfectionism: an ABC approach

Adaptability:

Be flexible and 'let go' in an attempt to stop control-freak tendencies and allow for more flexibility within lessons. The best lessons tend to be those involving spontaneous teaching and learning experiences, fascinating discoveries and explorations.

Be kind:

Treat yourself like you would a good friend and try to give yourself a break more regularly. Add more self-care strategies to your day and try not to punish yourself. There are lots of self-care ideas in Part 2 where I address the practical ways to look after yourself. Take brain breaks if you are tired and can't think straight rather than battling on. Set strict time limits to complete tasks and stop once the time is up. You will notice that frequent breaks rejuvenate you and give you a fresh mindset.

(Continued)

162 A PERSONAL PLAN FOR WELLBEING

Table 6.1 Continued

Related sections of the book/Steps	Question to reflect upon	Your notes	Any related actions/targets/celebrations
		Celebrate: Notice and rejoice what went well and learn to aim for 'good enough', especially on those days when you are tired and overwhelmed. Remember that perfection is not possible. **Delegate:** Allocate tasks to others, if this is appropriate, and collaborate with colleagues so you can share resources and planning. **Establish priorities:** Ask yourself questions like 'What really matters here?' so that you maintain perspective.	
Step 9: Your lifestyle choices	Do I allow myself sufficient rest? Do I have an environment that is conducive to good quality sleep? Do I feel good after a meal? Do I eat foods that give me a variety of nutrients and provide the bursts of energy that I need? Do I get enough exercise? Do I do exercise that I enjoy and look forward to?	Reflect upon your lifestyle choices in relation to the quality of and how much you sleep, what and how much you eat and the exercise that you do. Compelling evidence has been found, for instance by Firth et al. (2019), that suggests that certain lifestyles factors can influence the mental health of an individual. Indeed, Dr Batman (2020), International Occupational Health Advisor for Virgin, believes that 'over 70% of your risk of becoming ill or the ability to treat illness is due to lifestyle'. As you read Chapter 4, write notes about any changes you feel are important to implement into your life....	

Chapter 5

Step 10: <u>Expressing gratitude and acknowledging staff</u>

At present, do I show people in my life that I am grateful for them?
Have I any colleagues at school that I value and that add to the enjoyment of my job?
What do these colleagues offer me?
Do I support other staff at school?
How do I show my gratitude when someone helps me or offers me support?
Who do I value the most at work and why?
What strengths do I possess? What support do I offer to others? How could I improve?

Can you think of a way that suits your personality, and will resonate with staff, that you can show your appreciation of the hard work and commitment from colleagues?

If you are not a school leader, then consider who, and how, you can show appreciation. Maybe this will be something small like popping a chocolate bar into someone's pigeon-hole or writing a note and leaving it on a colleague's desk.

Write notes about how you can bring about a sense of belonging and gratefulness within your workplace....

Step 11: Support network for a school leader

Who do I feel most comfortable with at school?
Why do they make me feel comfortable?
How do I feel when I ask for help from others?
Do I find it easy to ask for support at work?

After reading about the sources of support that I suggest for you as a school leader, reflect upon who you would go to in times of need. If you are not a school leader, then consider who your support networks are, both in and out of school.
Write down a list of your available support networks....

as a school leader, focus and a list of actions to consider. Please print off Table 6.1 and 6.2 from my website and add your own notes.

- Writing a staff wellbeing policy

Working on the creation of a staff wellbeing policy will allow you to see wellbeing as an ongoing and dynamic process. When educational professionals were asked if they had a staff wellbeing policy, in the ESP's 'Teacher Wellbeing Index' (2019:66),

- 43% said they didn't know if they had one or not,
- 13% said no, they had no policy,
- 44% said yes, they had a policy (this had risen from 36% in 2018).

This shows that 56% either don't know or don't have a staff wellbeing policy yet, and so it is possible that more than half of schools have no staff wellbeing policy currently. Your school can, therefore, be ahead of the game if you decide to create one now. Alternatively, you could update a pupil wellbeing policy by adding a staff focus or add to your Diversity and Inclusion Policy to include a staff wellbeing section. It can act as evidence for Ofsted, if they visit and ask about the wellbeing support in your school.

The policy can start small and be worked on as ideas and strategies are being discussed by staff. To develop a policy, it is important to start with practice first and not policy first, for instance, printing off a staff wellbeing policy from a website that has been designed for a different school will not be appropriate or personal enough for your school.

With this in mind, the HEP paper (2017:40) listed some creative ideas for school leaders to reflect upon, which I believe could form the beginnings of a personalised wellbeing policy for a school:

- Create a vision or ethos statement for wellbeing to display in your school
- Approve core values with the staff, pupils and community
- Embed the values...(to) thread through all school activities—the curriculum, assemblies, behaviour management, reward systems, liaison with families
- Find out the signature strengths of the pupils and teachers, and work towards having a strengths-based school.

Table 6.2 An action plan for school leaders

Actions	Thoughts about the action
1) Find out what the term 'wellbeing' means to your staff	
By using one of recommended audience participation tools (see the 'Useful resources'), you could collect an anonymous word cloud of what wellbeing means to all of your staff. This could form the beginning of discussions around the change that needs to be instigated so that teacher wellbeing is supported using a personal approach.	
2) Assess staff wellbeing	
Is it appropriate for you to ask all of your staff to complete my 'How's your wellbeing?' assessment (Chapter 2) during a staff training session? You could design a survey to gauge the wellbeing of your staff and personalise it so that you are asking the most pertinent questions. These forms could be completed anonymously so that you can assess how the wellbeing of your staff is in general terms. Refer to the mental health continuum model for teachers (Figure 2.1) to keep an eye on your own, and colleagues, mental health in case it dips. The mental health continuum model for teachers could be displayed in the staff room.	
3) Use the Steps to Success	
The Steps to Success could be used in staff training or to facilitate a short discussion about teacher wellbeing in your weekly staff meetings.	

(Continued)

Table 6.2 Continued

Actions	Thoughts about the action
4) Set up wellbeing working groups or peer-support groups	Change does not happen without collaboration and commitment. Is it possible to gather together a working group in your school so that they can begin to look at wellbeing for your unique school? Alternatively, could you use distributed leadership where the school staff are divided into focus groups according to the area of wellbeing that they will focus upon? E.g. one group could look at wellbeing and marking, work/life balance or creating an up-to-date wellbeing policy for the school etc. Peer-support groups could be formed for those that feel as if they would like to meet to discuss any area of wellbeing that they choose. This should be emphasised as a safe space to offload but that it is a two-way process whereby staff are not there as experts but merely to offer a 'listening ear' and perhaps to share strategies that worked for them. If you wish for the process to be more formal, then staff can be recruited to form working groups in order to focus upon an area of change. These could constitute volunteers and ideally will be representatives for the following: an NQT, a middle leader, an early career teacher, a lunchtime supervisor, an administrators or school office manager, a cleaner, the SENCo, a governor, perhaps a parent, the Head or Deputy or Assistant Head etc. Encourage your staff to engage in 'blue-sky thinking' and then to delve into what change is possible in realistic terms. It is fine to start with small changes with a view to what you want to achieve for the big picture. Be patient because real change takes time. Be aware that some of your staff may be averse to change and have a fear of things changing despite the positive outcomes. It might be unanimous that staff would prefer for the Headteacher not to be involved in the change groups (or Headteachers may prefer not to attend). This may be so that staff do not feel prohibited from sharing their thoughts because the Headteacher is present at a meeting. Staff may find it helpful to discuss everything and only share the negative points with the Headteacher if there are a majority of staff feeling the same way. This is often less detrimental for a Headteacher who might find it hard to listen to negative comments and not take them personally when only a minority of staff feel this way. This process is rarely plain sailing as it can include setbacks and personality clashes among staff, but it does produce a renewed sense of community and common purpose prevails, as Rogers (2012:16) refers to this as the 'we're all in the same boat' feeling. These meetings should never constitute an attack or a change to mindlessly moan without the talk of positivity and what is already working as well as the change that needs to occur. The meetings should focus on uncovering issues around wellbeing but in a positive and diplomatic way. It's important to be willing to let go of old habits that no longer serve your staff or the children. Ideally, consulting a 'critical friend' from another school can work well so that an objective viewpoint and outside perspective about the changes decided upon can be considered and reflected upon. They may offer insights, especially around barriers that may exist.

WHAT IS MY PERSONAL PLAN FOR WELLBEING   167

Recruit a Designated Mental Health Lead (DMHL)	
Allocate one or more staff member to fulfil the role as Designated Mental Health Lead or wellbeing facilitator. This person should be willing to undertake this role and also be given time out of the classroom to develop this role and oversee wellbeing using a whole-school approach. This person could check on the actions set by the working groups and regularly provide updates on the progress being made towards the goals that were set by each group. Currently, it is not mandatory to have a DMHL in schools; it is only shared as a recommendation for schools.	
Create a staff wellbeing policy and/or WAPs	
Focus upon creating a wellbeing policy for your particular school. It may align with the Pupil Wellbeing Policy or it may stand alone. See the section in Chapter 6 about writing a wellbeing policy, and the considerations to make: 1) Form a working group 2) Vision statement 3) Staff survey 4) Statements that summarise the school's priorities and values 5) Measure the impact 6) Future improvements 7) Support available 8) Urgent crisis Decide whether it is appropriate for your staff to create Wellness Action Plans.	
Use the Teachers' Standards for Wellbeing	
Display the Teachers' Standards for Wellbeing (Figure 6.1) on your staffroom wall as a reminder of how important your wellbeing is.	

Actions to take to create a staff wellbeing policy

1) Working group
   Form a working group to meet to discuss how best to proceed.
2) Vision statement
   Decide upon a vision statement that best describes the unique approach to staff wellbeing in your school; it should illustrate the philosophy that all staff have around their wellbeing. By using a mind-map format, like Figure 5.1: Employee Wellbeing Tree, you can collect words that are important to your staff as a starting point for your vision statement.
3) Staff Survey
   You may also like to create a staff survey using an online tool (See Useful resources) that can be completed by all staff to collect ideas about what should be included in the staff wellbeing policy so that it represents the views of everyone.
4) Statements that summarise the school's priorities and values
   Produce from this survey about three statements that detail your school's approach to staff wellbeing, for example, 'We discuss our mental health needs with each other and respect everyone, not stigmatising or discriminating against anyone.' Include within this what the school already does well, and the teacher wellbeing initiatives already planned for.
5) Measure the impact
   Explore how your school's staff wellbeing progress could be evaluated or the impact measured.
6) Future improvements
   List any improvements planned for the future to address staff wellbeing.
7) Support available
   List the local and national support available that is deemed to be most helpful for you staff.
8) Urgent Crisis
   Provide details of the steps that would be taken in a crisis situation where a staff member was in crisis or struggling with severe mental health issues (see the below sections for ideas).

Wellness Action Plans (WAPs) for staff

If you have a wish for a strong focus and proactive approach to staff wellbeing in your school, or there is an overarching need for action to be taken, you may like to encourage your staff to create a Wellness Action Plan (WAP)—this should not be compulsory, though. A WAP is a confidential agreement between a staff member and a school leader to promote staff wellbeing; confidentiality is only broken in exceptional circumstances like if there is deemed to be a risk of harm. You can find some examples, and a template of a WAP in the Mind resource (see Useful resources). A WAP constitutes a two-way process and helps school leaders to develop in awareness about the wellbeing needs of their staff and the type of environment each staff member needs in order to stay well. The existence of a WAP can make a staff member feel listened to, cared for and heard.

Again, your approach to a WAP should be personalised according to your school and should not be a laborious process for either the staff member or the school leaders.

Elements to consider that could be included in a WAP are:

- Individual wellbeing approaches, for example, use of a peer wellbeing buddy.
- Signs of stress and triggers, for example, parents evening or public talking.
- Appropriate support for that person to alleviate their stress, for example, exercise or meditation.
- Potential actions if they become unwell, for example, contacting a member of their family.
- An agreed time to review the WAP, for example, every four months.

Tips for school leaders and staff if wellbeing becomes severely low

A small proportion of staff may experience low wellbeing where it is not appropriate to support them in the ways I have suggested so far, as their wellbeing needs are more severe. Obviously, the support is dependent on the particular needs they present with, but here are a few ideas for your consideration of where to signpost such staff members onto:

1) Specialist, professional support from a GP or psychiatrist (perhaps for medication such as beta-blockers or anti-depressants). It takes a while for anti-depressants to have a noticeable effect. They work in a patchwork pattern where the sufferer sometimes feels worse before they feel better.
2) Talking therapies work well in conjunction with medication, such as Cognitive Behavioural Therapy (CBT), Dialogic Behavioural Therapy (DBT) or Acceptance Commitment Therapy (ACT). These treatments encourage you to explore and challenge your cycles of negative thinking. I particularly find that ACT could prove helpful for a teacher, as it encourages a reflection on your values. It may help to recall your values and use these, and the memory of why you chose teaching as a driving force.
3) Try complementary therapies, if you can afford this. Some people find herbal remedies such as St John's Wort or homeopathy useful, although this should only be on the advice of your GP. Others find massage, meditation, yoga, dance therapy, art therapy, acupuncture, reflexology or reiki helps to lift their mood and support general wellbeing.
4) Attend a local support group or online forum so that you can mix with others to avoid the feeling that you are alone.

Supporting a member of staff who is experiencing crisis

McBrearty (2019:4), the CEO of ESP, commented in the 2019 'Teacher Wellbeing Index', that:

> Teachers tend towards the stoic, and usually wait until crisis point before accessing support. This is simply not sustainable, let alone desirable.

A theme that has occurred time and again in this book is the need to have a proactive approach to your wellbeing to share your struggles and to ask for help. Completing the 'Steps to Success' should focus you to plan for your personal wellbeing needs to avoid it dipping so low that you are eventually in crisis. However, this section deals with how a manager can help if mental health staff issues are extreme. A survey (Mental Health Foundation,

2016) revealed that 20% of people have attended work with suicidal thoughts, therefore signifying that any employer needs to have some foresight into how best to deal with a mental health crisis.

- Be mindful of your responsibilities for all employees and how the low wellbeing of one member of staff is impacting on others.
- If a staff member is in crisis, withdraw them to a quiet place and talk calmly to them.
- Suggest that they use the support networks available to them (this may be family and friends). Suggest they contact their GP for an immediate appointment, or a local mental health team.
- If a staff member needs emergency help, use the NHS helpline (call 111) or call an ambulance (999).

> *Do you remember the story I told you about my experience with a young girl on the bridge? Let me finish this now…*
>
> *I left the story where I had disclosed my own previous suicidal feelings and the young girl had asked me, 'Do you feel better? Do you still feel like you want to die?' I answered as honestly as I could to this and replied 'Yes, I do still have bad days, but I also have many moments of joy which allow me to carry on. I have found ways of coping with the pain.'*
>
> *The thought of brighter days seemed to lighten her mood slightly and she said, 'Thank you for stopping, you can leave me now'.*
>
> *I contemplated leaving her. I thought about the student that I had kept waiting for over half an hour by now. However, when I considered everything that I had learnt about suicide, I knew that I couldn't leave her like this, even though she was promising me that she felt better. She must have picked up on these thoughts because she begged, 'Please don't phone the police. My parents will be so angry with me.' I had left my phone in the car, which was only a few steps away, but I knew that if I left her side to go to my car, there was a chance she would jump. Thankfully, just at that moment another car stopped by the motorway bridge and a kind woman wound down the window of her car and mouthed to me 'Are you okay?' I shook my head and mouthed back 'Call the police, please.' I saw her retrieve her phone from her handbag and make the call. She then got out of her car and joined me by the young girl's side. We were all bitterly cold and I could see the young girl's hands were blue and still shaking as she clasped her suicide note. It still took us about 20 minutes to convince the young girl to walk away from the bridge railings.*

> She became angry when we explained that the police would arrive soon, but we told her that we had done this because we care and that she needs expert assistance. Eventually, we managed to persuade her to travel up the road to the kind lady's farmhouse to sit in her warm kitchen by the fire and talk some more. The police and paramedics arrived at the farmhouse and I was in awe of the way the police officer dealt with her and the empathy and understanding he showed; he admitted that he had experienced difficulties with his mental health in the past, and this again seemed to resonate with the young girl.
>
> That night I was touched to receive a text from the young girl that thanked me and said that I had saved her life that day. She also encouragingly said that the support she had received from Accident and Emergency at the hospital had really helped. I was relieved that my decision to call the police had been the right one.

Reintegrating a member of staff back to work after absence

My personal opinion is that sending a 'get well card' to a person who is on a leave of absence due to mental health reasons is appropriate, as it shows the same consideration that you would give to a person recovering from a physical illness. The approach that school leaders take when managing a staff absence sends messages about a school's values. A warm, empathetic approach impacts on the individual but also has a far-reaching impact on all staff.

If a member of your staff is absent from work, then it is crucial that you keep in touch with them so they do not feel forgotten or isolated. Maintaining contact with them will allow them to return to work more easily. As well as offering reassurance and keeping them informed about any work-related matter they wish to discuss, a 'return to work' plan should be created. This could be informal but should encourage their personal reintegration back to school, including whether a phased return is necessary etc. When the staff member returns to work, it is crucial that you meet with them on their first day back. This meeting should ideally build trust and facilitate a smooth transition back to duties. A reevaluation date should be fixed at this meeting so that the staff member can share their continued wellbeing progress or any challenges they are still experiencing.

Teachers' Standards for Wellbeing

The Teachers' Standards for Wellbeing is my reinterpretation of the Teachers' Standards (DfE, 2011), but with a focus on wellbeing. I have designed this document, mirroring the Government's version, to emphasise and enhance how important it is to have a central and preliminary focus on your wellbeing as a teacher even before striving to understand the skills of learning and teaching.

I intend to use the Teachers' Standards for Wellbeing with student teachers who are at the beginning of their journey, but they are just as relevant for experienced teachers that may benefit from remembering to always consider their wellbeing first. The 'preamble' could be seen as a motto that I feel all teachers should recite regularly. I recommend that this document is displayed in corridors and the staff room to act as a reminder of how important our wellbeing is (Figure 6.1 can be downloaded from my website).

Useful resources

- To collect anonymous ideas from your staff, I recommend the use of Padlet (https://padlet.com/) or Mentimeter (https://www.mentimeter.com/)
- Useful online tools to create a survey include: Survey Monkey (www.surveymonkey.com) and Google Forms (https://docs.google.com/forms/
- The charity, Education Support Partnership, offers help and support for anyone working in education.
  Phone: 0800 0562 561 (Freephone, 24 hours a day, 7 days a week)
  Text: 07903 341229
  Email: support@edsupport.org.uk
  Website: www.Educationsupportpartnership.org.uk/chat-support
- Shout is a crisis text-line that operates 24/7. All you need to do, if you are in crisis, is text the word 'Shout' to 85258.
- The details for the Samaritans can be found at https://www.samaritans.org/
  You can contact them 24/7 by phoning 116 123, or by emailing them at jo@samaritans.org, or write to them:
  Chris Freepost RSRB-KKBY-CYJK
  PO Box 9090 Stirling,
  FK8 2SA

174 A PERSONAL PLAN FOR WELLBEING

♥ Looking after me

Teachers' Standards for Wellbeing (Allies, 2020)

PREAMBLE

Although teachers should make the education of their pupils their first concern, they should also have their own wellbeing as a top priority. Without their health and wellbeing, teachers are unable to achieve their highest possible standard and maintain their full potential at work. Teachers, therefore, need to be honest about how they are feeling and show integrity towards the wellbeing of others; they should have strong subject knowledge related to wellbeing, keep their knowledge and skills of wellbeing strategies up-to-date and operate in a self-critical way using a personal approach to wellbeing; they should forge positive professional relationships by discussing wellbeing and showing acceptance and a non-judgemental attitude towards the wellbeing needs of colleagues.

PART ONE: WELLBEING

A teacher must:

1 Set high expectations for themselves which motivate and inspire

- Establish an environment that is conducive to wellbeing in their home and classroom
- Demonstrate consistently positive attitudes, values and behaviour towards your wellbeing for 90% of the time. The remaining 10% is for naughtiness.

2 Promote good wellbeing outcomes

- Be accountable for their wellbeing and take ownership of it
- Be aware of why they are focusing on their wellbeing and plan for this so they can adequately support their class
- Guide pupils to reflect on their own wellbeing emerging needs
- Encourage pupils by being a role model to take a responsible and conscientious attitude to their own wellbeing.

3 Demonstrate good subject knowledge in wellbeing

- Have a secure knowledge related to wellbeing by reading Part 1 and 2 of Allies (2020) *Supporting teacher wellbeing: A practical guide for primary teachers and school leaders*, Routledge
- Address any misconceptions that arise in relation to wellbeing
- Maintain an interest and value in reading research in wellbeing

4 Plan for your own wellbeing

- Impart knowledge and develop understanding of wellbeing
- Plan to incorporate wellbeing strategies consistently and regularly into pupils' out-of-class activities
- Contribute to the design and provision of a healthy school that has the wellbeing of children and staff at its heart.

5 Adapt wellbeing strategies to respond to themselves and the needs of pupils

- Use wellbeing strategies that suit their unique lifestyles
- Have a secure understanding and awareness of their wellbeing and the knowledge of how a range of factors can inhibit their wellbeing and the wellbeing of their class
- Know how to adapt to the problems that may arise related to wellbeing
- Show empathy and understanding of other people's wellbeing issues.

6 Make accurate use of wellbeing strategies and assess their effectiveness

- Know and understand how to assess wellbeing strategies
- Reflect upon the personal effectiveness of wellbeing strategies and respond to feedback from their body and mind
- Set targets for their own wellbeing and identify their steps to wellbeing success

7 Manage your behaviour effectively to ensure wellbeing

- Have clear rules and routines for wellbeing and take responsibility for promoting good wellbeing around them in accordance with the school's wellbeing policy
- Have high expectations of wellbeing and establish a personal plan for wellbeing with a range of strategies
- Feel empowered about their own wellbeing and reward the ability to work towards wellbeing
- Act decisively when necessary to protect their own wellbeing and that of others

8 Fulfil wider wellbeing responsibilities

- Make a positive wellbeing contribution to the wider life and ethos of the school
- Develop effective relationships with colleagues, knowing how and when to draw on expert advice and specialist support for wellbeing
- Encourage all staff to learn more about wellbeing and incorporate this learning into their continued professional development
- Communicate effectively with parents with regard to pupils' wellbeing

PART TWO: PERSONAL WELLBEING CONDUCT

A teacher is expected to demonstrate consistently high standards of personal and professional wellbeing conduct. The following statements define the behaviour and attitudes which set the required standard for wellbeing conduct throughout a teacher's career.

- Teachers uphold public trust in the importance of staff and pupil wellbeing, within and outside school, by:
  o treating pupils and colleagues with dignity and building relationships rooted in mutual respect around wellbeing for all
  o having regard for the need to safeguard pupils' wellbeing in accordance with statutory provisions
  o showing tolerance of and respect for everyone's right to wellbeing

Figure 6.1 The Teachers' Standards for Wellbeing: Guidance for trainee teachers, school leaders, school staff and governors.

- Mindful Employer: 'Mindful Employer aims to increase awareness of mental health at work and provides easily accessible information to organisations and supports for staff who experience stress, anxiety, depression or other mental health conditions.'
  Phone: 01392 677 064
  Email: info@mindfulemployer.net
  Website: www.mindfulemployer.net
- Garland, L et al (2019) Ten Steps towards school staff wellbeing, Anna Freud National Centre for Children and Families, available at: https://www.annafreud.org/what-we-do/schools-in-mind/resources-for-schools/ten-steps-towards-school-staff-wellbeing/
- Mind, *How to support staff who are experiencing a mental health problem* (Resource 4), Available at: www.mind.org.uk/work You can find information about Wellness Action Plans here and a website that provides guidance to help employees take care of themselves.

Takeaway messages

1) COVID-19 pandemic and teacher wellbeing

At the time of writing, schools are recovering from the aftermath of the COVID-19 health crisis. This event led to a heightened need for school staff to focus on wellbeing as they adapted to lockdown, home-schooling, and social distancing and coped with tensions between their personal and work circumstances. School leaders were forced to embrace uncertainty and grapple with the overwhelming government guidance and daily amendments about how to respond to this unprecedented situation. Schools collectively braved these strange times, creating, I hope, a sense of unity amongst staff. Engaging in a healthy dose of self-care was never so important following the long and tiring days educational staff experienced; the preparation involved in an Ofsted visit seemed nothing compared to this!

As I work towards the publication of this book, I am reassured that it highlights many areas that are being suggested by experts as the way forward for staff to recover from the pandemic. In particular, by:

- Ensuring that schools encourage discussions around all their personal stories related to the pandemic, including the open sharing of triumphs and useful coping strategies, traumas, and loss in a safe and supportive way. Non-judgemental listening and compassion are key here, as always.
- Developing more control over your mind to manage any anxiety or worry around the changing educational landscape.
- Prioritising your time and getting plenty of fresh air and exercise, along with engaging in regular mindfulness practices.
- Buying into the need for supervision and for it to be made available to teachers. Indeed, the Education Support Partnership (ESP) plan to pilot a project that will provide online peer-support and telephone supervision for school leaders.
- Monitoring how happy school staff are as the government commits to publishing findings alongside introducing a wellbeing charter. For more information go to: https://www.gov.uk/government/news/extra-mental-health-support-for-pupils-and-teachers

2) Thank you!

I would like to thank you, the reader, for buying this book and thereby making wellbeing a main concern. I hope you found that working through 'Steps to Success' gave you focus and the impetus to make changes if they were required, both individually and within your school.

I would love to hear about the work you are doing in schools around staff wellbeing, especially if it is to share the impact of anything I have suggested in this book.

I would also like to hear your stories and any feedback you have for me about any issues/points I raised in this book, especially if you have any suggestions for ways that I could improve.

My email is s.allies@worc.ac.uk and my website is www.supportingteacherwellbeing.wordpress.com. I'd love to hear from you. Look after yourselves and each other.

REFERENCES

Adams, R., & Stewart, H. (2018). *Damien Hinds pledges to help teachers overwhelmed by excessive workload.* Available at: https://www.theguardian.com/education/2018/jul/20/hinds-pledges-to-help-schools-reduce-teacher-stress-to-retain-staff (accessed 18.2.2020).

Anna Freud National Centre for Children and Families. (2019). *Supporting staff wellbeing in schools.* Available at: https://www.annafreud.org/media/7653/3rdanna-freud-booklet-staff-wellbeing-web-pdf-21-june.pdf (accessed 10.8.2019)

ASCL. (2020). *Improving Ofsted inspections.* Available at: https://www.ascl.org.uk/ASCL/media/ASCL/News/Press%20releases/Ofsted-survey-analysis-March-2020.pdf (accessed accessed 14.6.2020).

Bajorek, Z., Gulliford, J., & Taskila, T. (2014). *Healthy teachers, higher marks? Establishing a link between teacher health and wellbeing and student outcomes.* London: The Work Foundation.

Bandura A. (1995). *Self-efficacy in changing societies.* Cambridge, UK: Cambridge University Press.

BBC News. (2019). *A Teacher's Story- eat, sleep, teach, repeat.* Available at: https://www.bbc.co.uk/news/av/uk-england-hampshire-46738445/a-teacher-s-story-eat-sleep-teach-repeat (accessed 20.2.2020).

REFERENCES

Bethune, A. (2020). *The importance of kindness in schools.* Available at: https://www.educationsupport.org.uk/blogs/importance-kindness-schools (accessed 28.2.2020).

Boogren, T. (2018). *Take time for you: Self-care action plans for educators.* Bloomington, IN, United States: Solution Tree Press.

Boorman, S. (2009). *NHS health and wellbeing review: Interim report.* London: Department of Health.

Braiker, H.B. (1989 December). The Power of Self-Talk. *Psychology Today,* 23–27. Available at: http://www.monaghanwib.com/wp-content/uploads/2016/05/The-Power-of-Self-Talk.pdf (accessed 18.2.2020)

Briner, P. R., & Dewberry, D. C. (2007). *Staff wellbeing is key to school success: A research study into the links between staff wellbeing and school performance.* London: Worklife Support.

Buckingham, M., & Goodall, A. (2019). *Nine lies about work: A freethinking leader's guide to the real world.* London: Harvard Business Review Press.

Burch, D., & Penman, V. (2013). *Mindfulness for Health: A practical guide to relieving pain, reducing stress and restoring wellbeing.* London: Piatkus.

Burns, J. (2019). *Ofsted boss Amanda Spielman warns mentioning exams ups pressure.* Available at: https://www.bbc.co.uk/news/education-48258797 (accessed: 18.2.2020).

Cambridge Dictionary. (2019). *Self-esteem.* Available at: https://dictionary.cambridge.org/dictionary/english/self-esteem (accessed 19.5.2019)

Carney, D.R., Cuddy, A.J.C., & Yap, A.J. (2019). Power Posing: Brief Nonverbal Displays Affect Neuroendocrine Levels and Risk Tolerance. *Psychological Science,* 21(10): 1363–1368.

Carr, K. (2017). *Teacher wellbeing: Little things mean a lot.* Available at: http://education.nswtf.org.au/education23/news-and-features-4/teacher-wellbeing-little-things-mean-lot/ (accessed 25.2.2020).

Charney, D. (2012). *Resilience: The science of mastering life's greatest challenges.* Cambridge, UK: Cambridge University Press.

Cirillo, F. (2020). *Do more and have fun with time manamgement.* Available at: https://francescocirillo.com/pages/pomodoro-technique.

Deloitte MCS Ltd. (2017 October). *Monitor Deloitte- Mental Health and Employers: The case for investment, Supporting Study for the Independent Review.* Available at: https://www2.deloitte.com/content/dam/Deloitte/uk/Documents/public-sector/deloitte-uk-mental-health-employers-monitor-deloitte-oct-2017.pdf (accessed 17.2.2020)

Department for Education (DfE). (2011 updated 2013). *Teachers' Standards Guidance for school leaders, school staff and governing bodies*. Available at: https://assets.publishing.service.gov.uk/government/uploads/system/uploads/attachment_data/file/665520/Teachers__Standards.pdf (accessed 22.3.2019).

Department for Education. (2012). *Statistical first release*. Available at: https://assets.publishing.service.gov.uk/government/uploads/system/uploads/attachment_data/file/223587/SFR15_2013_Text_withPTR.pdf

Department for Education (DfE). (2016). *Reducing teacher workload*. Available at: https://assets.publishing.service.gov.uk/government/uploads/system/uploads/attachment_data/file/593913/6.2799_DFE_MB_Reducing_Teacher_Workload_Poster_20161213_print.pdf (accessed 14.6.2020).

Department for Education (2018, updated 2019). (2019). *Ways to reduce workload in your school(s): Tips and case studies from school leaders, teachers and sector experts*. Available at: https://www.gov.uk/government/publications/ways-to-reduce-workload-in-your-school-tips-from-school-leaders (accessed 2.1.2020)

Department for Education. (2019a). *Summary and recommendations: teacher well-being research report*. Available from: https://www.gov.uk/government/publications/teacher-well-being-at-work-in-schools-and-further-education-providers/summary-and-recommendations-teacher-well-being-research-report (accessed 2.1.2020)

Department for Education. (2019b). *Teacher recruitment and retention strategy*. Available at: https://assets.publishing.service.gov.uk/government/uploads/system/uploads/attachment_data/file/786856/DFE_Teacher_Retention_Strategy_Report.pdf (accessed 2.1.2020)

Dweck, C. S. (2008). *Mindset: The new psychology of success*. New York: Ballentine Books.

Education Support Partnership-Teacher Wellbeing Index. (2019). Available at: https://www.educationsupport.org.uk/resources/research-reports/teacher-wellbeing-index-2019 (accessed 12.1.2020)

Ericsson, K. A. (1990). Peak Performance and Age: An Examination of Peak Performance in Sports. In P. B. Baltes & M. M. Baltes (Eds.), *Successful aging: Perspectives from the behavioural sciences* (pp. 164–195). Cambridge, UK: Cambridge University Press.

Estyn. (2013). *The impact of teacher absence*. Wales: Her Majesty's Inspectorate for Education and Training in Wales.

Exley, S. (2015). *Three-quarters of new teachers have considered quitting, survey reveals.* Available at: https://www.tes.com/news/three-quarters-new-teachers-have-considered-quitting-survey-reveals (accessed 17.2.2020)

Ferguson, D. (2019). *I sold my house, came out as gay and stood as Green councillor: life after headteaching.* Available at: https://www.theguardian.com/education/2019/jul/23/sold-house-came-out-as-gay-stood-as-a-green-councillor-life-after-headteaching (accessed 17.2.2020).

Fiore, N. (2007). *The now habit: A strategic program for overcoming procrastination and enjoying guilt-free play.* New York: TarcherPerigree.

Fujita, H. (1997). *A study on the culture of teaching and teacher professionalism in Japan.* Tokyo: University of Tokyo

Galton, M., & MacBeath, J. (2008). *Teachers under pressure, NUT.* London: Sage

Glazzard, J. (2018). *Pupil progress is being held back by teachers' poor mental health.* Available at: https://www.teachwire.net/news/pupil-progress-is-being-held-back-by-teachers-poor-mental-health (accessed 17.2.2020)

Glazzard, J., & Rose, A. (2019). *The impact of teacher wellbeing and mental health on pupil progress in primary schools.* Available at: https://www.leedsbeckett.ac.uk/-/media/files/schools/school-of-education/teacher-wellbeing--pupil-progress-research.pdf?la=en (accessed on 18.2.2020).

Global Burden of Disease. (2019). Life Expectancy and Disease Burden in the Nordic Countries: Results from the Global Burden of Diseases, Injuries, and Risk Factors Study. *Lancet,* 4(12), 1958–1972.

Greenfield, B. (2015). How Can Teacher Resilience be Protected and Promoted?. *Educational and Child Psychology,* 32, 52–68.

Hanson, R. (2009). *Buddha's brain: The practical neuroscience of happiness, love, and wisdom.* Oakland, CA: New Harbinger Publications.

Harding, S., Morris, S., Gunnella, D., & Ford, T. (2019). Is Teachers' Mental Health and Wellbeing Associated with Students' Mental Health and Wellbeing? *Journal of Affective Disorders,* 242, 180–187.

Health Education Partnership (HEP). (2017). *A PSHE and wellbeing framework.* Available at: http://healtheducationpartnership.com/resources/HEP_Primary_PSHE_Framework.pdf (accessed 8.2.2020)

Health and Safety Executive (HSE). (2017). *Mental health conditions, work and the workplace.* Available at: http://www.hse.gov.uk/stress/mental-health.htm (accessed 5.12.2019)

Health Survey for England (HSE). (2014). *Mental health problems.* Available at: https://files.digital.nhs.uk/publicationimport/pub19xxx/pub19295/hse2014-ch2-mh-prob.pdf (accessed 26.1.2020).

HSE. (2019). *Tackling work-related stress using the Management Standards approach A step-by-step workbook.* Available at: https://www.hse.gov.uk/pubns/wbk01.pdf (accessed 4.2.2020).

Hodge, K. (2015). *Workload forcing new teachers out of the profession, survey suggests.* Available at: https://www.theguardian.com/teacher-network/2015/jan/27/workload-new-teachers-work-life-balance (accessed 17.2.2020).

Hunt, M.G., Marx, R., Lipson, C., & Young, J. (2018). No More FOMO: Limiting Social Media Decreases Loneliness and Depression. *Journal of Social and Clinical Psychology,* 37(10), 751–768. Available at: https://doi.org/10.1521/jscp.2018.37.10.751 (accessed 15.3.2020).

Independent. (2018). *Teachers under 'great' pressure from pupils and parents, admits education secretary.* Available at: https://www.planstaffnow.co.uk/news/teachers-under-great-pressure-from-pupils-and-parents-admits-education-secretary (accessed 18.2.2020)

Kell, E. (2018). *How to survive in teaching without imploding, exploding or walking away.* Bloomsbury.

Kondo, M. (2014). *The Life-Changing Magic of Tidying: A simple, effective way to banish clutter forever.* Vermilion

Kitchen, R. (2018). *Warning over teacher stress crisis in Yorkshire schools.* Available at: https://www.yorkshirepost.co.uk/news/latest-news/warning-over-teacher-stress-crisis-in-yorkshire-schools-1-9284686 (accessed 18.2.2020).

Lightfoot, L. (2020). *Outstanding primary schools fail Ofsted inspections under sudden rule switch.* Available at: https://www.theguardian.com/education/2020/feb/04/outstanding-primary-schools-fail-ofsted-inspections-under-sudden-rule-switch (accessed 2.2.2020)

Luke, I., & Gourd, J. (2018). *Thriving as a professional teacher.* Abingdon: Routledge.

Maslow, A. (1943). A Theory of Human Motivation. *Psychological Review,* 50(4), 370–396.

McBrearty. (2019). *In the foreword for the education support partnership-teacher wellbeing index.* Available at: https://www.educationsupport.org.uk/resources/research-reports/teacher-wellbeing-index-2019 (accessed 12.1.2020)

McGonigal, K. (2013, June). *How to make stress your friend* (K. McGonigal, Performer) TED Global, United States.

McLeod, S. A. (2014). *Carl Rogers*. Available at: Simply psychology: https://www.simplypsychology.org/carl-rogers.html (accessed 12.8.2019)

Mehrabian, A. (1981). *Silent messages: Implicit communication of emotions and attitudes.* Belmont, CA: Wadsworth

MHFA England. (2016). *MHFA Line Managers' Resource*. MHFA. Available at: https://cdn.mentalhealthatwork.org.uk/wp-content/uploads/2018/07/05111111/line_managers_resource.pdf (accessed 6.2.2020).

Montgomery, C., MacFarlane, L., & Trumpower, D. (2012). Student Teacher Stress and Exercise. *Proceedings of ASBBS, 19*(1). Available at: http://asbbs.org/files/ASBBS2012V1/PDF/M/MontgomeryC.pdf

Morrison McGill, R. (2014). *A 5 point plan for teacher wellbeing*. Available at: https://www.teachertoolkit.co.uk/2014/07/03/5-point-plan-for-teacher-wellbeing/ (accessed 6.2.2020).

Mulder, P. (2017). *Eisenhower matrix*. Available at: https://www.toolshero.com/personal-development/eisenhower-matrix/ (accessed 20.2.2020).

National Resilience Institute webpage. (2020). *What is resilience?* Available at: https://nationalresilienceinstitute.org/what-is-resilience/ (accessed 1.2.2020).

NHS. (2020). *Exercise*. Available at: https://www.nhs.uk/live-well/exercise/ (accessed 1.2.2020)

Office of National Statistics (ONS). (2017). *Suicide by occupation, England: 2011 to 2015*. Available at: https://www.ons.gov.uk/peoplepopulationandcommunity/birthsdeathsandmarriages/deaths/articles/suicidebyoccupation/england2011to2015 (accessed 17.2.2020).

Ofsted. (2011). *Best practice in safeguarding in colleges*. Available at: https://assets.publishing.service.gov.uk/government/uploads/system/uploads/attachment_data/file/417603/Best_practice_in_safeguarding_in_colleges.pdf (accessed 15.6.2020).

Ofsted. (2019a). *Education inspection framework*. Available at: https://www.gov.uk/government/publications/education-inspection-framework (accessed 15.2.2020)

Ofsted. (2019b). *School inspection update*. Available at: https://assets.publishing.service.gov.uk/government/uploads/system/uploads/attachment_data/file/772056/School_inspection_update__January_2019_Special_Edition_180119.pdf (accessed 15.2.2020)

Ofsted. (2019c). *Summary and recommendations: teacher well-being research report.* Available at: https://www.gov.uk/government/publications/teacher-well-being-at-work-in-schools-and-further-education-providers/summary-and-recommendations-teacher-well-being-research-report (accessed 4.2.2020).

Ofsted. (2020). *Responses to post-inspection surveys: state-funded schools.* Available at: https://www.gov.uk/government/publications/responses-to-post-inspection-surveys-state-funded-schools (accessed 14.6.2020).

O'Leary, M., & Price, D. (2016). Peer Observation as a Springboard for Teacher Learning, O'Leary, M. (Ed.), *Reclaiming lesson observation: supporting excellence in teacher learning* (pp. 114–123). Abingdon: Routledge.

Oswald, A.J., Proto, E., & Sgroi, D. (2015). Happiness and Productivity. *Journal of Labour Economics, 33,* 789–822.

PSHE Association (funded by the DfE) (Updated for 2019). (2019). *Teacher guidance: teaching about mental health and emotional wellbeing.* Available at: https://www.pshe-association.org.uk/system/files/Mental%20Health%20guidance%20online%20version%20%28Updated%20July%202019%29.pdf (accessed 1.2.2020)

Pillen, M. Beijaard, D., & den Brok, P. (2013). Tensions in Beginning Teachers' Professional Identity Development, Accompanying Feelings and Coping Strategies. *European Journal of Teacher Education, 36*(3), 240–260

Porter, T. (2019). *Ofsted's framework: what it means for pupil mental health.* Available at: https://kevinhempstedcounsellor.com/articles/f/ofsteds-framework-what-it-means-for-pupil-mental-health (accessed 12.2.2020).

Raedeke, T. D., & Smith, A. L. (2009). *The Athlete burnout questionnaire manual.* Morgantown, WV: Fitness Information Technology.

Rath & Harter. (2010). *Wellbeing: The five essential elements.* Gallup Press

Rogers, B. (1992). *Supporting teachers in the workplace.* Australia: Financial Times Management

Rogers, B. (2012). *The essential guide to managing teacher stress.* Gosport: Pearson Education Limited.

Rogers, T. (2018). *'We must save our NQTs from early burnout – they need time, space and, above all, trust.* Available at: https://www.tes.com/news/we-must-save-our-nqts-early-burnout-they-need-time-space-and-above-all-trust (accessed 17.2.2020).

Sacks, O. (2017). *The river of consciousness.* Picador

Sammons, A. (2019). *The Compassionate Teacher: Why compassion should be at the heart of our schools*. John Catt Educational Ltd.

Selye, H. (1976). *The stress of life*. New York: McGraw-Hill.

Smith, H., & McGrandles, A. (2018). *The impact of mental health and wellbeing on effective learning and teaching: A practical guide for those responsible for learners*. Swan and Horne.

Santry. (2018). *Three in 10 teachers using medication to cope with pressure of job*. Available at: https://www.tes.com/news/three-10-teachers-using-medication-ope-pressure-job (accessed 17.2.2020)

Speck, D. (2019). *Exclusive: DfE finally admits teacher supply has 'worsened'*. Available at: https://www.tes.com/news/exclusive-dfe-finally-admits-teacher-supply-has-worsened (accessed 17.2.2020)

Steele, P. (2012). *The procrastination equation: How to stop putting things off and start getting stuff done*. New York: Harper Perennial.

Stoeber, J., & Rennert, D., (2008). Perfectionism in School Teachers: Relations with Stress Appraisals, Coping Styles, and Burnout. *Anxiety, Stress, & Coping*, 21(1), 37–53

Teach Thought Staff. (2016a). *A teacher makes 1500 educational decisions a day*. Available at: https://www.teachthought.com/pedagogy/teacher-makes-1500-decisions-a-day/ (accessed 13.2.2020)

Teach Thought Staff. (2016b). *A teacher makes 1500 educational decisions a day*. Available at: https://www.teachthought.com/pedagogy/teacher-makes-1500-decisions-a-day/ (accessed 3.4.2019)

Thich, N. H., & Weare, K. (2017). *Happy teachers change the world: A guide for cultivating mindfulness in education*. Berkeley, CA: Parallax Press.

Thorley, C. (2017). *Not by Degrees*. London: Institute for Public Policy Research (IPPR).

Tolle, E. (2016). *The power of now: A guide to spiritual enlightenment: A guide to spiritual enlightenment (20th Anniversary Edition)*. London: Yellow Kite.

Tzu, L. (2018). *Sayings of Lao Tzu*. Singapore: A & D Publishing.

Warwick, I., & Mooney, A. (2009). *National Healthy Schools Programme: Developing the evidence base*. London: Thomas Coram Research Unit: University of London.

Wax, R (2016). *A mindfulness guide for the frazzled*. London: Penguin Books Ltd.

We are teachers website article, (2020). *Should teachers take mental health days?* Available at: https://www.weareteachers.com/mental-health-days/ (accessed 18.2.2020)

Whippman, R. (2016). *The pursuit of happiness: And why it's making us anxious.* London: Hutchinson.

Whittaker, F. (2019). *Recruitment and retention strategy pledges £130m for new teacher induction.* Available at: https://schoolsweek.co.uk/recruitment-and-retention-strategy-pledges-130m-for-new-teacher-induction/ (accessed 18.2.2020)

WHO. (2014). *Mental Health: A state of wellbeing.* World Health Organisation. Available at: http://www.who.int/features/factfiles/mental_health/en/ (accessed 4.11.2019).

WHO. (2005). *2005 report 'Promoting Mental Health'*. Available at: https://apps.who.int/iris/bitstream/handle/10665/43286/9241562943_eng.pdf?sequence= (accessed 4.11.2019)

Wilson, S. (2019). *First we make the Beast Beautiful: a new conversation about anxiety.* London: Corgi.

Work Stress Network. (2020). *Work stress.* Available at: http://www.workstress.net/sites/default/files/stress.pdf (accessed 13.3.2020).

INDEX

Page numbers in *italics* refer to figures, those in **bold** indicate tables.

'absentee-ism': 'presentee-ism' and 22, 34; rate and impact of 29–30
Acceptance Commitment Therapy (ACT) 91, 170
acknowledging staff 142
action plan for school leaders 157–158, **165–167**
active listening skills 138, 140, 155–156
Allies, S. *33*, 174, 176
Anna Freud National Centre for Children and Families 128–129, 154
anti-inflammatory foods 108
anxiety, description and symptoms of 45–47
anxiety and depression 45, 47, 83; Statutory Assessment Tests (SATs) 85–87; sources of support 169–170; *see also* depression, perfectionism, self-esteem
asking for help 85–86
assessment of wellbeing 4–5, 54, **55–57**

Association of School and College Leaders (ASCL) 26
Association of Teachers and Lecturers (ATL) 21

Bajorek, Z. 29
Bandura, A. 102
BBC News 25, 84
behaviour management 93, 121, 135–136
Bethune, A. 71
Boogren, T. 18, 99
Bousted, M. 79
breakfast ideas 111
breaks 5–6; and breaking down jobs 81
Briner, P. R. 28, 29
Buckingham, M. 41
Burch, D. 53, 120
burnout 39–41, 96, 98, 100

Cambridge Dictionary 87
Carney, D. R. 93
Carr, K. 99

Chair of Governors 151
changing role of teachers 24–25
Charney, D. 102
'check-ins' 5, 32, 43, 117; pupils 121; staff 142
Cirillo, F. 81
classroom calm 120–121
coaching/mentoring 133–134
Cognitive Behavioural Therapy (CBT) 46, 170
colleague support 35, 88, 132
colleagues: socialising with 70–71; see also peer coaching/mentoring, peer support
communication; see listening/active listening skills, open dialogue
Compassion Focused Therapy (CFT) 53
complementary therapies 170
confidence see self-esteem
confidentiality 140, 169
continued professional development (CPD) 134–135
COVID-19 pandemic 175–176

Deloitte MCS Ltd 34
Department for Education (DfE) 23–24; absenteeism 29–30; main elements of wellbeing 13; PSHE Association paper 120–121; Reducing Teacher Workload 76, 79; Teachers' Standards 96, 98
depression: description and symptoms 47–48; Seasonal Affective Disorder (SAD) 107; see also anxiety and depression
designated mental health lead (DMHL) 133
Dewberry, D. C. 27, 29
Dialogic Behavioural Therapy 170
diet see food
disclosure 139
distractions, avoiding 81
Dweck, C. S. 98

early-career teachers see work-life balance
early retirement of school leaders 150
Education Inspection Framework (EIF) 26–27
Education Support Partnership (ESP) 152; see also Teacher Wellbeing Index (ESP)
Eisenhower method of procrastination 81
emails 73
emotional contagion 31
Employee Assistance Programmes (EAPs) 128, 130
employee wellbeing tree 137, 137
environment: school 131–132; sleep 105
Equality Act 141
Ericsson, K. A. 81
Estyn Report 29–30
Executive Head 152
exercise 112–116

FAB PRO acronym 80–82
Ferguson, D. 151
'Fika' times 70, 71
Film Club 74
Fiore, N. 80
fluid intake 105, 109
FOMO acronym 87
food 106–110; meals 110; promoting sleep 104
forgiveness 80
fun 92
Future Learn 135

Galton, M. 12, 24
Glazzard, J. 15–16, 29–31, 54
Global Burden of Disease report 107
Goodall, A. 41
Golden Week 130
Gourd, J. 12

government guidance and perspectives 23–24, 133; see also Department for Education (DfE)
GPs 170, 171
gratitude, expressing 142
Greenfield, B. 102
growth mindset 98

Hamilton Trust 76
Hanson, R. 53
Harding, S. 29
Harter, J. K. 68
headteachers see school leaders
health care 130
Health Education Partnership (HEP) 128, 131, 164
Health and Safety Executive (HSE) 36; Management Standards 127
Health Survey for England 45
Hinds, D. 23–24
Hodge, K. 21
holidays 75
Hunt, M. G. 87

Independent 23
insomnia advice 104

job satisfaction 27, 142

Keates, C. 21, 24
Kell, E. 14–15
Kempsey Primary School Academy 146
Kitchen, R. 24
Kondo, M. 87

Lao Tzu 86
learning to say 'no' 19–20
lesson observation 94–95; by peers 133–134
lesson planning 75–76, 92
lifestyle choices 102–116
Lightfoot, L. 27
listening/active listening skills 137–139, 155–156

living by your values 91–92
local support groups 170
Luke, I. 12
lunch ideas 111–112

MacBeath, J. 12, 24
McBrearty, S. 170
McGill, M. 135
McGonigal, K. 42, 43
McGrandles, A. 34
McKeith, G. 106
McLeod, S. A. 155
macronutrients 107
marking 75, 79
Maslow, A. 18
meals 110
measurement of wellbeing 12–13
medication 170
meditation and mindfulness 51–52, 53, 116; see also mindfulness
Mediterranean diet 107, 109
Mehrabian, A. 155
mental health continuum 32–36, 33, 84
mental health days 86
Mental Health First Aid England 13
mental health first aiders (MHFA) 135
Mental Health Foundation 90, 170–171
mental health and wellbeing: changing role of teachers 24–25; definitions 11–12; Education Inspection Framework (EIF) 26–27; government guidance and perspectives 23–24, 133; measurement of 12–13; pressures of teaching 14–18; pupil perspective 31; and pupil progress 27–30; of school leaders 22–23; self-care, importance of 18–19; staff support role of school leaders 20–22; testing, consequences of 25–26; work and non-work impacts 13–14

mentoring/coaching 133–134
micronutrients 107
mindfulness 116–118; activities 118–119; meditation and 51–52, 53, 116; and negative thoughts/self-talk 48–51
minerals 107
modelling wellbeing 122, 150
Montgomery, C. 113
Moran, L. 24
morning routine 111
Mulder, P. 81
multiple roles of teachers 18–19

National Association of Headteachers 151
National Association of Schoolmasters and Union of Women Teachers (NASUWT) 21
National Children's Bureau 128
National Education Union (NEU) 79
National Foundation for Educational Research 79
National Hub for Supervision in Education 154
National Union of Teachers (NUT) 79
negative thoughts/self-talk 48–53
neuro-plasticity 53
Newly Qualified Teachers (NQTs) see work-life balance
non-work activities 72–73, 72
non-work impacts 13–14

observation see lesson observation
Office for National Statistics (ONS) 16
Ofsted 24; behaviour management 135–136; criticisms of 16, 100, 151; Education Inspection Framework (EIF) 25–27; school environment 131; school leader role 126–127
O'Leary, M. 133–134
online lesson plans 76

online support groups 170
open dialogue 136, *137*
Organisation for Economic Co-operation and Development (OECD) 79–80
organising 82; and 'letting go' 86–87
Oswald, A. J. 14
overworking 83
Oxford English Dictionary 11–12

panic attacks 47
paperwork see workload
parents 88–90, 143
Path of Progress (POP) planning format 77–78, *77*, *78*
peer coaching/mentoring 133–134
peer support 71
Penman, V. 53, 120
perfectionism 94–96; case study 62–63, 66; potential consequences of 98; strategies for dealing with 99–102; types and traits 96–98
personal plan: action plan for school leaders 157, 164, **165–167**; COVID-19 pandemic 175–176; reintegrating staff after absence 172; staff experiencing crisis 170–172; staff and school leaders experiencing low wellbeing 169–170; staff wellbeing policy 164, 168; steps to success 157, 164, **158–163**; Wellness Action Plans (WAPs) for staff 169
Personal, Social, Health and Economic Education (PSHE) 91, 120
phytochemicals 107
Pillen, M. 70
planning for sustained wellbeing: behaviour management 135–136; continued professional development (CPD) 134–135;

examples of good practice 143–148; expressing gratitude and acknowledgement 142; listening/active listening skills 137–141, 155–156; open dialogue 136, 137; peer coaching/mentoring 133–134; regular check-ins 142; school culture 132–133; school vision and environment 131–132; tips 143; whole-school approach 128–129, 131–132; year-round initiatives 129–130
Pomodoro technique 81
Porter, T. 25
positive focus 90–91
power poses 93
'presentee-ism': and 'absentee-ism' 22, 34; avoiding 142
pressures of teaching 14–18
Price, D. 133–134
prioritising tasks 81
procrastination 80–81
psychiatric support 170
pupil feedback 92
pupil perspective 31
pupil progress 27–30

Raedeke, T. D. 39
Rath, T. 68
Rayner, A. 23
Reducing Teacher Workload (DfE) 76, 79
reintegrating staff member after absence 172
Rennert, D. 96
repetition and retreat 118–119
resilience 101–102
responsibilities, waiving and delegation of 150
rest times 72
rewards 82
Rogers, B. 35, 85, 88, 132
Rogers, C. 87–88, 155

Rogers, T. 61–62
role models: school leaders 150; teachers 122
routines: and 'letting go' 86–87; morning 111; sleep 103

Sacks, O. 53
St John's Middle School Academy 144–146
Sammons, A. 53, 100
Sane 47
Santry, C. 21
Statutory Assessment Tests (SATs) 25, 28, 85–87
school-based strategies 54
school counsellor 148
school culture 7, 132–133; toxic 15–16
school environment 131–132
School Improvement Plan 135
school leaders: mental health and wellbeing of 22; resilience of 102; role of 20–22, 125–128; see also personal plan, planning for sustained wellbeing
school leaders, support for: causes of early retirement 151; from staff 149–150; network 153–154; sources 151–153; tips to minimise pressure 150
school vision and environment 131–132
scientific perspective: stress response 42–45, 44; threat-system and sooth-system 53, 100
Seasonal Affective Disorder (SAD) 107
self-care 99–101; importance of 5, 18; promoting sleep 103–106
self-efficacy 93, 102
self-esteem: definition and sources of 87–90; tips for building 90–93
self-talk/negative thoughts 48–43

Senior Leadership Team (SLT) 152–153
sharing feelings 85
sky-watching 119–120
sleep 103–106
SMILES trial 109
Smith, A. L. 39
Smith, H. 34
snacks 105, 112
social media use 87
socialising with colleagues 70–71
sooth-system, threat-system and 53–54, 100
specific, measurable, attainable, relevant and time-limited (SMART) 68
special days 130
Speck, D. 24
Spielman, A. 25
staff meetings 143
Staff Shout Out 91
staff support 20–22, 125–128; for school leaders 149–150
staff wellbeing policy 164, 167
Steele, P. 80
steps to success 4, 157–164, **158–163**; adding more pleasurable pursuits to your life 72–73; analysing fear and panic 47; audit your time 73–74; expressing gratitude and acknowledgement 142; learn to say 'no' 19–20; lifestyle choices 102–116; no one is perfect! 99; previous wellbeing strategies 12; regular check-ins 5; stop and drop negative thoughts 51–53; support network for school leader 153–154
Stoeber, J. 96
stress 36–38; and burnout 39–31, 96, 98, 100; causes and recognition of 37–38; definition of 36; pressures of teaching 14–18; science of 42–45, 44; igns of 37–38

STRIPES acronym 103–106
suicide/suicidal thoughts 16, 100; intervention 137–138, 170–172
supervision 153–154
SWIM acronym 150

talking therapies 170
Teach Thought Staff 18
teacher roles: changing 24–25; modelling wellbeing 122; multiple 18
Teacher Wellbeing Index (ESP) 5, 7, 15, 27, 29, 170; exercise 113; meditation and mindfulness 116; resilience 102; school leaders 149; staff wellbeing policy 164; work-life balance 61, 66–67
Teacher and Workload Survey Report 79
Teachers' Standards: DfE 96, 98; for wellbeing 173, 174
team-building exercise 69
teamwork 71
technology use 104
testing, consequences of 25–26
Thich N. H. 48, 116
Thorley, C. 12–13
threat-system and sooth-system 53, 100
time audit 73–74
time management: school leaders 150; *see also* work-life balance
Tolle, E. 51
toxic school culture 15–16
Trello 82
trying to understand 86

values, living by your 91–92
VERSE acronym 141, 153
vitamins and minerals 107

Weare, K. 116
WeAreTeachers.com 85
Wellbeing Buddy 71
wellbeing strategies, previous 12
Wellness Action Plans (WAPs) 169

whole-school approach 128–129, 131–132
Wilson, S. 113
work and non-work impacts on wellbeing 13–14
work-life balance: case studies 62–66; challenge of achieving 66–70; importance of 41–42, 61–62; overworking 83; planning 75–78; tips 70–75
workload: challenging 74–75, 79–80, 143; procrastination 80–82
Work Stress Network 36
work success and self-esteem 88–90
World Health Organization (WHO) 11, 13, 39

year-round initiatives 129–130
Yorkshire Post 129

Printed in Great Britain
by Amazon